CW00376332

First published 2009 by Mountain Media

Mountain Media
Old Glen Road,
Newtonmore,
Inverness-shire PH20 1EB

www.mountain-media.co.uk

© Mountain Media 2009

Text by Cameron McNeish for Mountain Media

Photography by Richard Else for Mountain Media

Maps drawn by Allyson Shields

Editorial and project management by Project One Publishing Solutions, Crieff
www.projectonepublishing.co.uk

Design and layout by The Partnership Publishing Solutions Limited, Glasgow
www.the-pps.co.uk

Cover design by e i d e t i c, Edinburgh

Set in 11.5pt ITC Garamond Light / ITC Bernhard Modern / Aldus Light

Printed by Scotprint, Haddington

ISBN-13: 978-0-9562957-0-5

Contact details, accommodation and travel information are correct at the time of going to press. Significant changes will be posted on **www.mountain-media.co.uk**.

The **Leave No Trace** principles are reproduced by kind permission of the Leave No Trace Center for Outdoor Ethics, Boulder, CO, USA.

While every effort has been made to contact copyright holders Mountain Media apologises for any who have been inadvertently overlooked.

 The paper used in this book is FSC accredited.

CONTENTS

ACKNOWLEDGEMENTS

Our names may be on the front cover but the book, and the television programme it came from, would never have been completed without a large supporting cast.

David Harron, Editor, Television Sport at BBC Scotland, has given us huge support and initially suggested the north-west of Scotland, the land of his forefathers, for our long walk. We hope this book will be the encouragement he needs to take his walking boots with him the next time he visits his family home in Lochinver. Likewise our thanks are also due to our Commissioning Editor at BBC Scotland, Ewan Angus. It's thanks to him that *The Adventure Show* is the only prime-time programme of its sort on a mainstream channel.

Dominic Scott, a talented fell runner, hillwalker and climber, was our patient cameraman and bravely coped with the rain and the midges and the wild camps. His superb camera work gave us the material to make a great film.

Paul Tattersall and John Lyall were our much valued safety officers and we're sorry they didn't have the opportunity to put their undisputed mountain talents to better use – although they both made excellent tripod carriers!

Individuals like John MacKenzie, James Morrison, Bruce Sandison, Donald Fisher, Jan Mackenzie, Jim Johnston, Angela Mackay and Grant McNicol were all extremely patient, and well-informed, interviewees. Looking after our every need were the staff at the Kyelsku Hotel, the Scourie Hotel and the Tongue Hotel – no-one can say Sutherland lacks good places to stay and eat!

Gina McNeish, Cameron's wife, made sure he enjoyed his usual creature comforts on their initial recce walk of the route (she carried the whisky flask) and Margaret Wicks not only produced the television programme but organised all the filming trips and interviews with magnificent aplomb. Laura Hill, also in the Triple Echo office, fought valiantly to balance the books.

Sincere thanks are due to Tony Wayte and Fiona McDonald of Project One who made sure this book was put together exactly as we wanted, and to Jack Geddes and Eleanor McCallum whose design skills have created a book that looks better than we could ever have hoped.

Finally, our deep thanks go to the people of Sutherland who guarantee that this magnificent corner of Scotland will never again be thought of as 'empty lands'.

Cameron McNeish and Richard Else, *Newtonmore, June 2009*

FOREWORD

You will probably have heard of the Aboriginal Australian vision of the 'Songlines'. According to this vision – a theology of a sort – the landscape of Australia is criss-crossed by a network of tracks and paths, which were laid down during the creation of the world. Each of these paths has a corresponding song, whose every note corresponds to a significant feature of the path – a rock outcrop, creek, or eucalypt that it passes, say, or a corner that it turns. To sing, according to this vision, is therefore to find one's way. Storytelling is indivisible from wayfaring, and the whole landscape is thick with plots and narrative. You just need to know how to sing them up.

The vision of the Songlines is often contrasted with white settler accounts of Australia's interior from the mid-nineteenth-century, which saw the desert as a *terra nullius*, an empty land, 'a Climax of Desolation', as the explorer Daniel Brock put it in 1845. Where the white settlers saw an absence of meaning in the landscape, the Aboriginals saw meaning's abundance. Where the white settlers perceived the desert only laterally, the Aboriginals perceived it deeply.

Many other indigenous cultures practise a version of the Songlines. The nomadic Chemehuevi of the Mojave Desert, for instance, navigated the wide expanses of arid rock and sand using songs. The songs gave the names of places in geographical order, and the place names were descriptive or evocative, such that a person who'd never been to a place might recognise it from the song. 'How does that song go?', in Chemehuevi, means 'What is the route it travels?' Similarly, in Navajo culture of the American south-west, place-names that index specific landmarks are told in sequence to form stories or 'verbal maps' describing routes of travel for people to follow. Guidelines in the non-bureaucratic sense.

It seems to me that Cameron McNeish and Richard Else have begun, with their television programme *Sutherland – The Empty Lands?* and this book, to create a songline for Sutherland. They have summoned, in order to banish, the old heresy of Sutherland as a *terra nullius*. Instead, they have found and proved it to be a landscape that is superbly rich in history, teeming with life – human and natural – and wealthy with stories, from the Archaean era through to the contemporary. I hope that Cameron's trail becomes, over the years, a well-trodden path, and that thousands of subsequent pedestrians stride out along it, walking up – waking up – Sutherland's songs.

Robert Macfarlane, *May 2009*

INTRODUCTION

Early winter snow throws the summit ridge of Quinag into sharp relief, while away to the south-west lies the largest village in the region – the fishing community of Lochinver.

It had been an extraordinary few days. In the company of one of Scotland's best-known anglers I fished for brown trout in the waters of Loch Haluim, as idyllic a setting as anyone could wish for; I climbed the castellated turrets of Ben Loyal, with views that stretched from Orkney to the Cairngorms; I learned why sheep are still vitally important to the Highland economy from a female shepherd who reckons she has the best job in the world; and I waded out into the shallows of the Kyle of Tongue with a woman who had made the highly unusual career change from hairdresser to oyster farmer.

But the highlight of my time in Sutherland took place in the cosy, comfortable surroundings of the Tongue Hotel in the company of a young man who had just celebrated twelve months as Scotland's Young Chef of the Year. He prepared some of the oysters for me, oysters that hours earlier had basked on the salted foreshores of the Kyle. With a glass of chilled Chardonnay on hand I slid those Kyle of Tongue oysters down my throat, before tucking into a fillet of beef from the nearby Castle of Mey farm, served on a haggis cake and accompanied by local winter vegetables.

And all this took place in a land of supposed barren bog-lands, where the chefs reputedly go home at seven in the evening and where the midges fly around in ever-decreasing circles looking for someone to bite. This is an area of northern Scotland that is perceived by many otherwise sensible folk as being a little bit like the Arctic – cold, barren and unpeopled since the Clearances.

A landscape that stretches as far as the eye can see.
Looking south from Loch Haluim.

Lying on the very edge of Europe, its west and north coasts blown and battered by the vagaries of the wide Atlantic, Sutherland has been historically known as the Empty Lands. Perhaps that term should be the Emptied Lands, for this northern county was once significantly more populous than it is today, but the politics and economics of the 18th and 19th centuries decreed that sheep were more valuable than people.

Under the flaming torches of notorious estate factors like James Loch and Patrick Sellar, carrying out the orders of the Duchess of Sutherland, the people were banished to the coastlines. The tears of the tides have left their mark here and it's not difficult, in the light of images from the Balkans in the 1990s, to visualise the ghostly lines of humanity, bowed under the weight of their possessions, picking their way north, as they did in 1819, abandoning their Strath Naver homes and fields behind them for an unknown future. Or others, like the grandfather of Assynt crofter John MacKenzie, being displaced

Many examples of cleared villages can be found in the infamous Strath Naver.
This is Grumbeg with Ben Klibreck dominating the distant skyline.

from the green lime-rich fields of Inchnadamph for the rocky coastal fringe of Assynt where the piles of rocks, cleared by hand to create rough fields and pastures, can still be seen, and wept over, today.

One Tongue resident told me that even today it can be uncomfortable for people called Sutherland to live in their eponymous county. When I mentioned we had a family called Sellar living in my village she looked horrified and said: "Oh my God!"

In 1852 a report on the Highland Clearances in the *London Times* concluded with the remark: "It is thus clear that the Highlands will all become sheepwalks and shooting grounds before long."

Prophetic words, but what now? Lamb prices have reached an all-time low and few sporting estates, if any, are economically viable. Many appear to be bought as playthings for wealthy absentee landlords who only want to shoot a few deer and catch a few salmon. What will the next turn of the wheel offer to the lost villages of Sutherland?

Depopulation of the Highlands has long been a political hot potato, a problem with few apparent answers. Young people leave the crofts and the villages to go to university in the south, or to seek work. Traditional houses are bought up as second homes – the typically Scottish 'but'n'bens' are no longer dilapidated bothies where families rough it for the odd holiday but three- and four-bedroom bungalows, complete with manicured gardens and nice views to the hills. Those that are not bought as holiday homes are taken up by retired couples, eager to spend their autumn years 'in the country'. Many don't even make it through the first winter.

For generations, travelling in the far north required patience and perseverance. There are many examples of the old single track road – this one cuts across the peat lands west of Tongue.

> **"** *... local people have discovered a new purpose and meaning, freed from the traditional feus and pressures of tenancy.* **"**

The result of this is that young people can't afford to get on the first rung of the housing ladder in places like Lochinver or Scourie or Durness or Tongue. Others inherit the family croft but have to live elsewhere, where the work is more appealing than gathering in a few sheep, digging a few vegetables and living by the harsh rule of the weather.

But as I discovered, Sutherland, like much of Highland Scotland, is re-inventing itself. People are returning to the glens, not in great numbers yet, but as the tensions and strife and economic uncertainties of urban Britain become increasingly intolerable, more and more folk are searching for an alternative lifestyle. Angela Mackay is no newcomer – her family name has been synonymous with this landscape for countless generations. Once she was the local hairdresser – today she's a highly accomplished oyster farmer. And the oysters have a major plus point – they don't talk back to you. Others are newer to the area, like the Danish artist who finds inspiration in the colours and shades of her newly adopted home, or the sea kayaker who earns a living from building drystone walls.

Many local people have discovered a new purpose and meaning, freed from the traditional feus and pressures of tenancy. The Assynt crofters made history with the first community buy-out of land their families had farmed for generations. Their story is an inspiring one, and led the way to similar buy-outs on Eigg, in Knoydart and in the Western Isles, where young people are realising that crofting is not necessarily an anachronism, but a way of life that allows them to remain in the glens and villages where they were born. People like 16-year old James Morrison can speak with passion and eloquence about the possibilities and potential for crofting, and offer wise advice for the politicians whose rules and over-regulation he believes are threatening this way of life almost out of existence.

During three seasons spent in Sutherland – spring, summer and autumn – I walked the old routes between Lochinver and Tongue and talked at length to crofters, hoteliers, fishermen, politicians and all those who come to take recreation here on the mountains, on the lochs and rivers, on the open seas, and in the caves of Inchnadamph. In that time, I discovered a new momentum at force, a fresh impetus, an energy that would hint at a positive future for these northern lands.

I've known the hills of Sutherland for many years and I've happily accepted the fact that its chameleon-like landscape has the ability to lift your spirits to soaring heights, or plunge them into total despair. Walk in towards Suilven on a dour, grey day when the midges and clegs feast on your bare flesh and the sodden ground wants to suck you under and you'll know what I mean by despair. But there are other times, more often than you'd dare believe, when Sutherland wears her wilderness gown with poise and subtlety; when this northern landscape, considered by many to be remote and harsh, boggy and battered by the elements, visually softens into a palette of the most delicate shades and hues. Or go there in a not infrequent riot of sunset colour and experience a pageant that can be gloriously brash and extravagant. There is no doubt that this region of northern Scotland has an uncompromising beauty, a glorious and lavish splendour that has the ability to reduce you to tears.

A typical scene repeated throughout Sutherland – vast tracts of deserted land where human hands have had little impact.

WALKING THE EMPTY LANDS

Throughout the pages of this book we reveal a Sutherland that is rich in wildlife, natural resources and stimulating scenery; a region that was once greatly more populated than it is today and could be again; a region that belies its common perception as the Empty Lands.

In an attempt to understand the area, to get as close as possible to the land itself, I chose to walk across it, from Lochinver on the west coast to Tongue on the north coast. My journey took in the summits of Suilven, one of Scotland's most iconic mountains, Foinaven, the hill that every hill-bagger thought must be a Munro but isn't, and Ben Loyal, "the queen of Highland mountains", according to the *New Statistical Account* of 1840.

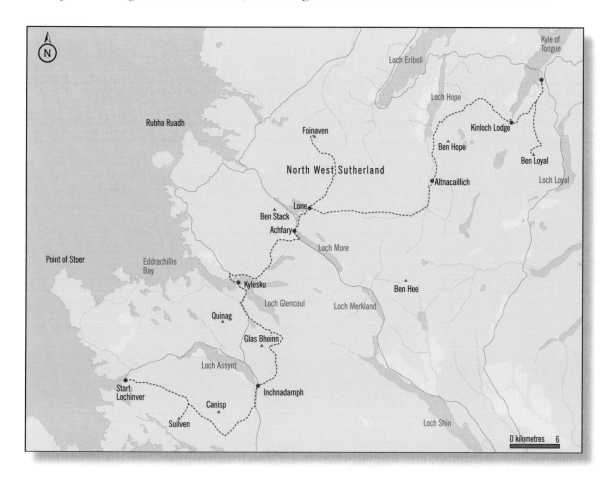

During the spring of 2008 I walked the route of the Sutherland Trail in its entirety with my wife Gina. On three nights we camped wild and on three nights we used a hotel. We walked about 130 kilometres in total and we could have camped wild each night, or climbed more fantastic mountains or stayed every night in some form of roofed accommodation.

Later that year, I visited the area several times more during the summer, and autumn with a BBC film crew to make the television documentary, *Sutherland – The Empty Lands?* The narrative of this book is made up from all those visits, plus the experiences of climbing the other hills of Sutherland, visits that have been made over the past 35 years.

Our route took us through south Assynt, over the shoulder of Canisp to follow the river through fields of yellow broom to Inchnadamph with its limestone caves and old stalkers' paths that tease out the contours and follow well-trodden yet sly lines up, through and over the hills to the Eas a' Chùal Aluinn overlooking the secretive waters of Loch Glencoul. This is the highest waterfall, at 200 metres, in the UK and it drains a vast wilderness of rocky crags, hummocks and hollows, each bowl caressing its own green-tinted lochan, which in turn gives birth to its own cascading stream, all harnessed by the steepening gradients into the roaring cataract that drops with frightening abruptness over the black, glistening crags of the Leitir Dhubh into the waters of the loch below.

From the waterfall we followed the eroded tourist track back to the main road at Loch na Gainmhich and then, tired and hungry, plodded along the longest stretch of road on the entire route – about six kilometres down the grassy verge, drawn by the prospect of a night in Kylesku, a tiny hamlet clustered round its pier, an old community that boasts one of the best hotels in the Highlands. No camping for us tonight – we fed on freshly made haggis and freshly caught langoustine, drank locally brewed beer and French wine, and slept in a comfortable bedroom that overlooked Loch Glencoul and Loch Glendhu – the waters of Kylesku of the Celtic song – lulled to sleep by the sounds of the surf and gently wakened in the morning by the cry of gulls.

Next morning, fortified by scrambled eggs and smoked salmon, we crossed the slender Kylesku Bridge and left the dancing waters behind. Our route now lay north and east, crossing the divide between Scotland's western seaboard, a land of hill, glen and

Autumn in the foreground; winter on the summit.
The bulk of Canisp seen from near Glencanisp Lodge.

deep-biting fiords and into the mountainous hinterland. It would be a few days until we reached the sea again at the Kyle of Tongue.

The hill track across the Reay Forest Estate between Kylestrome and Achfary climbs steadily away from Loch Glendhu beside a rosary of hill lochs that stretch away to the east towards the curiously named Meallan Liath Coire Mhic Dhughaill, which translates as 'the rounded hill of the corrie of Dougal's son'. What story lies behind that name? And what stories lie behind the ruckle of stone that is marked as a single shieling on the Bealach nam Fiann before the track drops down into the Achfary Forest and Lochmore Lodge?

A welcome landmark for the walker travelling from Kylesku to Achfary. This remote shieling marks the end of the high ground and the start of the descent to Lochmore Lodge.

" Meallan Liath Coire Mhic Dhughaill …
What story lies behind that name? "

Beyond Achfary we tramped along the road for a short distance before we left it to cross the river, past Loch Stack and the locked bothy at Lone and up to the saddle in the hills between the three Corbetts of Foinaven, Arkle and Meall Horn. We climbed Foinaven for the television programme, following a midge-ridden camp above Loch an Easain Uaine. Despite the biting bugs it is undoubtedly one of the best hills in the north, the veritable Queen of Sutherland.

After returning to Lone, we headed east, following a good track into Srath Luib na Seilich where we could see the U-shape of the Bealach na Fèithe. This high pass was the watershed of the route, the crossing of a divide, from the north-west coast, where the culture and ancient language is that of the Western Isles, into the land of the North, where the culture and language is more Orcadian. Put succinctly, the people of north-west Sutherland will go to Ullapool for their shopping, while the people on the east side of this bealach will gather towards Thurso. The regions are split by the high and the low, the north–south spine of Meall Horn, Foinaven, Cranstackie and Beinn Spionnaidh, and the fiord-like Loch Eriboll that bites into the land like a hungry shark.

We sensed the difference as we descended above the Abhainn Srath Coir' an Easaidh. The tang of salt air had gone – we were now in a parched land where the old trees, with little or no progeny, looked worn and tired. We were in deer forest where the land is managed with only two things in mind – the shooting of stags and salmon fishing.

Gobernuisgach Lodge and its manicured grounds came and went and we followed a fisherman's path north up Strath More to the broch of Dùn Dornaigil, one of Scotland's best surviving examples of a circular defensive tower of the Iron Age.

We camped at the foot of the Moine Path, the old peat road that runs over the north side of Ben Hope, below its formidable crags and buttresses, towards the Kyle of Tongue. It was our final camp of the trip. The weather deteriorated during the night, bringing rain and a brisk south-westerly wind. We took the peat road through the mist, eventually

Ben Loyal, often called the Queen of the Highlands, seen here from Lochan Hakel.

coming out of the cloud to be greeted by a forlorn and grey Kyle of Tongue. The multi-topped Ben Loyal flirted with us through the mists, appearing and disappearing in the cloud. Past Kinloch Lodge we took to the minor road for the last few miles to Kirkiboll and Tongue, where I enjoyed the delights of the excellent Tongue Hotel to toast a marvellous week on a route that I hope will become a popular one – the Sutherland Trail.

I guess if we had wanted to learn more about Sutherland we could have driven around the region, Richard taking photographs and me writing up my notes, talking to the people, enjoying the provender of the land, hearing the tales and the history, admiring the mountains and the coastline, before blasting off again in a cloud of CO_2 emissions for our next appointment. But essentially I'm a mountain bum, a wilderness enthusiast who can best understand such a landscape as this by walking through it and listening to its heartbeat, trying to read its small print, walking to its own rhythms.

Given the choice I would have probably walked between Lochinver and Tongue and, as much as possible, avoided folk. I've hiked trails in wilderness areas throughout the world that are simply devoid of people other than fellow wilderness backpackers, and I've always enjoyed the experience but on this occasion I was walking with a different purpose, dancing to a different tune.

Shepherd Jan Mackenzie working on one of her crofts in Strath Naver. She works both for herself and the local estate.

The Mackay clan have been integrally bound up with the history of Sutherland.
Several are buried in the churchyard at Balnakeil near Durness.

We were making a television documentary and I wanted to meet people en route and talk to them, interview them, interrogate them. I wanted to discover why they wanted to live here, or work here, or recreate here. I wanted to read the larger print – the history, the folklore, the politics, the perceptions and the ambitions. I wanted people to convince me that Sutherland was not the Empty Lands, and that the potential and the promise of this northern county was as rich as anywhere else. I wanted to get under the skin of the land …

On a good day – and there are surprisingly many – Sutherland can compare with anywhere in the world.
Sunset from the summit of Ben Stack, with hundreds of lochans giving this landscape its characteristic look.

I was intrigued to discover, at the end of my journey, as I basked in the luxury of the Tongue Hotel in front of an autumn fire with a glass of malt whisky in my hand, that the satisfaction and fulfilment of completing a long walk through wonderful landscapes had actually been enriched by the people I had met – the crofters, the cavers, the geologists and the climbers, the sea kayakers and the fly fishermen, the shepherds and the historians and all those who had helped us along the way. I had discovered that my rather narrow mountaineering perspective of the wild lands of Sutherland had been broadened and had developed, and my knowledge of a land I thought I knew fairly well had been widened. I also realised that many of my perceptions about traditional land use had been blown apart. When I eventually left Sutherland I knew I was leaving a tiny part of myself there, a glimmer of my own spirit left among the shining levels of the lochans and the luminous moods of the vast moorlands. Something tells me I'll never be a stranger there again …

> **" *A long walk through wonderful landscapes had been enriched by the people I had met.* "**

USING THE BOOK AS A GUIDE

Richard and I have been very aware that many readers will want to use this book to follow the actual route of the Sutherland Trail. That is why we've included trail information with each chapter detailing distances, maps, terrain and the actual step-by-step route.

However, we also felt it was important that we included information about some of the hills that are accessible from the trail, for those readers who want to climb as many of the hills from the trail as possible.

Canisp, Ben More Assynt and Conival, Quinag, Ben Stack, Arkle, Meall Horn, Ben Hope and others are all adjacent to the trail, so where possible I've written of my own experience of these hills taken from visits over a number of years.

I've also included details of some other areas that are close to the trail, such as the Bone Caves, which are important when describing the geology of Assynt, and the area furth of Tongue, like Strath Naver and its important associations with the Highland Clearances.

One of the most distinctive mountains in Scotland – Suilven. Although only 731 metres high, it rises majestically from the surrounding landscape to dominate the area around Lochinver.

For the unwary, the drive north from Ullapool could well shake up all the perceptions you've ever had about landscape, particularly if you come from the tidied, cultivated landscapes of the south.

Be prepared for a shock, and steady your mind in preparation for an assault on your arithmetical senses as you begin to juggle with and contemplate time-spans that most of us can't even begin to imagine.

A few minutes north from the neatly laid-out terraces and gift shops of the ferry port you'll drive over the brow of a hill and see the curved beach and bay of Ardmair. Beyond, commanding the north shore of the bay, is the long, weathered ridge of Ben More Coigach, an extensive wall of Torridonian sandstone, standing as a relic of one of the most ancient land masses in the world.

At the foot of the hill, under the sandstone, lies a platform of crumpled Lewisian Gneiss, said to be well over 1,000,000,000 years old, toughened by heat and pressure deep within the Earth's core. The hill's protective cap of Cambrian quartzite has long since gone, like many of its neighbours the victim of countless centuries of wind and frost. The bare bones of this venerable relic still rise straight from the sea to almost 750 metres, a wall nearly two kilometres long of seamed buttresses, gullies and cliffs, running slightly south of west to north-east, from Garbh Choireachain to Speicin Còinnich.

TRAIL INFORMATION

Lochinver to Inchnadamph

Map
Ordnance Survey 1:50,000 Sheet 15 (Loch Assynt, Lochinver and Loch Assynt)

Distance
24 kilometres / 15 miles (29 kilometres / 21 miles with ascent of Suilven)

Approx. time
8–10 hours (12–14 hours with Suilven)

Terrain
Good paths to Lochan Fada; rough ground on Suilven and crossing Canisp; easy walking beside River Loanan. If river is high, cross it by the bridge SW of Stronchrubie.

Route

Leave Lochinver from the main road to the S of the village (signposted). Follow road to Glencanisp Lodge, follow track behind the house and continue on bulldozed track past the bothy at Suileag to footbridge E of Lochan Buidhe. Cross bridge over river. Close to this point a cairn at the side of the track marks the rough path to Suilven.

Continue on path, cross another footbridge over the river and continue along the N shore of Loch na Gainimh, through the pass of the Allt a'Ghlinne Dhorca to Lochan Fada. Cross to S shore of the loch and follow path to the E end of the loch.

Leave the path now and climb in a NE direction over the shoulder of Canisp (no path). Continue in a NE direction and descend to the River Loanan N of Stronchrubie. Cross river (or use bridge further S) and follow river to Inchnadamph.

Accommodation

Culag Hotel, Lochinver: 01571 844270.

Inchnadamph Hotel: 01571 822202. Friendly staff, basic accommodation, local ales. Popular hotel with fishermen.

Inchnadamph Lodge Hostel: 01571 822218; enquiries@inch-lodge.co.uk. A first class independent hostel with a great range of facilities including drying room and laundry room. Highly recommended.

Public transport

A useful bus is the year-round Friday afternoon direct bus from Inverness to Lochinver (leaves 17:20, arrives 19:50).

Tim Dearman Coaches operate a daily bus from Inverness to Durness, calling at Lochinver, between May and September; 01349 883585; info@timdearmancoaches.co.uk.

There are regular trains between Inverness and Lairg and a Post Bus service between Lairg and Lochinver.

Suilven's appearance alters when seen from different angles. The eastern ridge is more pronounced when viewed from the crofting community of Elphin.

❝ *From this bed of bogs rise some of the most unlikely looking mountains in the world – Stac Pollaidh, Cul Beag and Cul Mor, Canisp and the most improbable of all, Suilven.* ❞

While that seaward wall is impressive, it's really only a front, a craggy facade that hides an intricate, complex system of peaks, ridges, corries and lochans. And beyond it, to the north, lies one of the most geologically complex areas of Europe – Coigach itself, Inverpollaidh, and the waterlogged, lochan-splattered district of Assynt, an ochreous mattress of knobbly rock and heather cut and divided by streams and rivers. From this bed of bogs rise some of the most unlikely looking mountains in the world – Stac Pollaidh, Cul Beag and Cul Mor, Canisp and the most improbable of all, Suilven.

Suilven, or Sula Bheinn, the Pillar Mountain, may not be a Munro or a Corbett but it's a remarkable mountain in every other respect. It's got bulk, it's got character, it's steep-sided and impressive, and its Torridonian sandstone tiers and proximity to the coast make it look twice the height it actually is. Suilven is the uncontested showpiece of Sutherland, and has its own chameleon tendencies. This hill not only changes colour and complexion depending on the angle of the sun, but it appears to change shape too, and dramatically so.

From the sea, and from Lochinver in particular, its western sentinel, Caisteal Liath, forms a huge rounded bastion of quartzite-capped sandstone. From Elphin in the east it can look like the Matterhorn, rising from its bedrock plinth of Lewisian Gneiss to a narrowing spire.

From Stac Pollaidh or Cul Mor in the south, its shape subtly changes again into a long, drawn-out sugarloaf, with an obvious depression in the middle – the Bealach Mor – the only apparent weakness in its fortress-like defences along a steep-sided and serrated ridge, some two kilometres in length.

The highest point, Caisteal Liath, the grey castle, lies at the north-west end of this ridge. There are two other summits – Meall Meadhonach (the middle round hill) is the central point of this ridge, while Meall Beag (the little round hill), lies at the south-eastern end.

Munros, Corbetts and Grahams

Over the years, various lists have been compiled to classify the mountains of Scotland according to their height. The first, and best-known, list was compiled by Sir Hugh Munro, who assembled the first definitive list of Scottish mountains over 3,000 feet, published as Munro's Tables in the *Journal of the Scottish Mountaineering Club* in 1891.

The **Munros** are a slightly contentious group, because Sir Hugh never set out any rules about distances or the amount of ascent and descent between adjacent high points. This has left the list open to a degree of interpretation, and every now and then, the Scottish Mountaineering Club undertakes a review of the Munros and promotes and demotes a few peaks. Some reclassification also takes place as a result of revised surveys of the mountains.

Munro's Tables are divided into Munros and Munro Tops – Munros are the main mountains, and Munro Tops are subsidiary summits which are over 3,000 feet but are not considered to be separate mountains in their own right.

Sir Hugh's original list had 283 mountains over 3,000 feet, and a further 255 Tops. The current list of Munros has 284 Munros and 227 Tops.

Corbetts are Scottish mountains with heights between 2,500 feet (762 metres) and 3,000 feet (914 metres). The list of Corbetts was compiled by John Rooke Corbett in the 1920s. Corbett lived in Bristol but spent much of his time walking in Scotland, and was the fourth person to complete the Munros in 1930 (and the first Englishman to complete the Munros). Corbetts are more clearly defined than Munros. In order to be classed as a separate hill, there must be a drop of at least 500 feet (152 metres) between each hill and any adjacent higher hill.

Corbett's original list showed 222 hills, and it has only been as a result of new surveys that the current total stands at 221 hills.

A third group of hills are the **Grahams**, which are Scottish hills between 2,000 feet (610 metres) and 2,499 feet (762 metres), with a drop of at least 150 metres (490 ft) between adjacent hills. The list was initially published in 1992 and later named Grahams after the late Fiona Graham. There are 224 Grahams.

Of course, all hillwalkers know that size isn't everything, and there are many Corbetts and Grahams which offer experiences every bit as good as anything that can be achieved on their bigger brothers.

SUILVEN EAST TO WEST

You can climb Suilven by a number of different routes, from Inverkirkaig in the south-west, from Lochinver in the north, or from Elphin in the east. Take your choice. The Sutherland Trail walker has the option of traversing the mountain from west to east, if starting the trail at Lochinver, but for the moment I'm going to describe the route I followed as my introduction to the mountain many years ago. A friend and I were dropped off by car in Elphin and picked up at the end of the day in Lochinver, and in between we enjoyed a marvellous through-route of some 26 wild and wonderful kilometres. This route also offers the adventurous opportunity of a scrambling ascent of the mountain's eastern prow, Meall Beag, and an east–west traverse of Suilven, a mountain day I'll never forget.

The dominance of Meall Beag's defences at the eastern end of Suilven gradually fades into something less threatening the closer you get to the hill – the angle of the eastern slopes lessen and it's with some relief that you realise that while the slopes are still very steep, the crags are eminently climbable. By threading together a variety of ledges you can scramble up to the broad summit of Meall Beag surprisingly quickly, but don't relax too soon – the main difficulties still lie ahead. Suilven doesn't surrender its crown quite so easily.

From Meall Beag the ridge narrows appreciably and you are greeted by a deep crack in the sandstone strata. Step across this fissure and continue until you reach a sudden and sheer drop with no obvious point of descent. This 30 metre drop poses a very serious obstacle, but it can be turned by descending steep ground on the north side of the ridge to where a faint line can be found traversing west into the dank and gloomy bealach below Meall Mheadhonach. From this dripping recess a faint path takes a zig-zag route up the steep slopes of Meall Mheadhonach from where more steep, rocky slopes eventually give way to grassy slopes dropping to the safety of the Bealach Mor. As if to offer some assurance, an ancient drystone dyke crosses the ridge at this point, pointing the way of the eventual descent route down a steep gully. If a wall can be built down the gully, it shouldn't prove too difficult to scramble down! In fact, the wall doesn't run down the slope too far, raising more questions about its curious purpose.

From the Bealach Mor an easy path leads to the summit of Caisteal Liath, a rounded dome of a place with breathtaking views of mountain, moor and sea. Enjoy the panorama, a visual feast from the mountains of Assynt in the north and east, the delectable outlines of Quinag and Canisp, the great massif that runs from Seana Braigh to Beinn Dearg in the east, south to the mountains of Inverpollaidh and west to the coastal hills of Coigach and Assynt.

Vast tracts of Sutherland seem spread out before you when you gain the summit ridge. This is the view north-west from Suilven.

The descent route follows the wall down the northern gully of the Bealach Mor. Pass the western outflow of Loch na Gainimh and find the stalkers' path, which also serves as the Sutherland Trail, crossing the Abhainn Clach Airigh and continues down the glen towards Glencanisp Lodge and the track to Lochinver.

I wanted to describe this glorious traverse of Suilven because it is one of the finest mountain excursions in Scotland and that's a bold statement to make for a hill that doesn't even make Corbett height, never mind make it onto the list of Munros. Suilven is a mere 731 metres high. Thomas Pennant, on his 17th century tour of the Highlands, called it the Sugar Loaf, a rather prosaic and uninspiring description of what is one of the most iconic mountains in Scotland.

LOCHINVER – THE START OF THE TRAIL

It was probably because of its iconic status that I chose Suilven as the starting point of my journey through Sutherland. But before you can climb Suilven you'll have to walk in to it, and for the purposes of hiking the Sutherland Trail you're best to begin in Lochinver. If you don't know this part of the world you might imagine a tranquil little fishing village at the mouth of the Inver River, a backwater of rural Highland life where retired couples go to set up their dream home or where crofters called Donald or Hamish or Morag live in tiny thatched cottages and where they keep a few sheep and grow small fields of potatoes and turnips. In reality, Lochinver is one of the largest villages in the north-west of Scotland. Built along the shores of Loch Inver, the village has for centuries been a safe haven for shipping on the west coast and the main traditional industries have always been fishing and fish curing.

Even today, fishing is an important source of employment and at the south of the village you'll find the busy modern harbour with its fish handling, processing and distribution centre, the busiest of the 102 harbours and jetties in the Highland Council area. Indeed, the base of the new headquarters of the Highland Council's harbour management team has recently moved from Inverness to Lochinver to be closer to what they describe as "the heart of the area's fishing industry".

Like other fishing ports on the west coast, Lochinver is today a shadow of its former self and many facilities like the Fisherman's Mission are now closed and sold off. The activity of previous years is replaced by increased dependence on tourism.

Once a major herring fishing port, Lochinver has managed to retain its importance even after the decline of the herring industry and it now ranks alongside Kinlochbervie to the north as one of the busiest fishing ports on this coast. Boats from all the coastal regions of Europe, especially Spain and France, are commonplace, with catches of many different species of fish being landed every day.

Here you'll find fishermen landing haddock, cod, plaice, monkfish, hake, lemon sole, prawns and lobsters, all caught in the crystal-clear waters of the North Atlantic. There are fresh shellfish too, with much of the catch flown to mainland Europe for sale the following day.

I don't imagine many folk would suggest the harbour area was pretty, but it certainly does have the compelling atmosphere that you'll find in sea ports the world over. The intoxicating smell of the sea blends with the stink of diesel and rotting fish, while the general hubbub of fish landings creates an unspoken expectancy and excitement. The foreign boats and flags create a cosmopolitan atmosphere where accents range from the soft lilt of the west highlanders to the broader strains of Aberdeenshire and Banffshire to the Gallic intonations of the southern Europeans.

In the 1990s Lochinver underwent a major renewal project. The harbour area was rebuilt and a new and much improved loading area was created. This new development involved blasting an area of several hectares out of the surrounding rock, an area that is still mostly undeveloped, with the exception of a new leisure centre.

Close by the harbour stands Lochinver's biggest building, the imposing Culag Hotel. This grand structure was built in 1873 as a shooting lodge and incorporated the buildings of an existing herring station. A fire devastated the structure in 1939 and it was largely rebuilt with many more recent extensions. It looks completely out of place in a working harbour, but I guess that's part of its charm. Another building that stands close to the harbour is the Royal National Mission to Deep Sea Fishermen which has recently closed.

Lochinver's other main industry is, of course, tourism. Few ports in the world can offer the kind of backdrop you'll find here with Suilven and Canisp dominating the skyline.

Situated in the centre of the village, the Assynt Visitor Centre provides tourist information for visitors and contains displays on the history, landscape and wildlife of Lochinver and Assynt, and is well worth a look. You shouldn't think of leaving the village without sampling one of the mouth-watering, freshly baked pies from the Lochinver Larder. Winner of numerous awards, the Larder attracts visitors from all over the country and in these days of fast food and processed food, it's heartening to know that every pie is baked on site. And what a bewildering range there is to choose from – cauliflower, broccoli and cheese; chicken curry; chicken and ham; savoury lamb; savoury mince; venison and cranberry; haggis, neeps and tatties; pork, apple and cider; steak and ale; and my own favourite, smoked haddock. Follow that with a sweet pie such as apple and blackcurrant, or rhubarb and strawberry, and you'll be more than ready to tackle the walk-in to Suilven – or you might just want to find a bed to lie down on for an afternoon nap!

The village has a wide range of facilities for locals and tourists alike. There are grocery stores, a butcher and a newsagent, as well as a bank, petrol station, post office and doctor's surgery and the recently built leisure centre. For the visitor, there are craft and gift shops as well as restaurants. There is hotel accommodation in the village and the surrounding area, as well as guest houses and bed and breakfast establishments.

I've always enjoyed my sojourns in Lochinver but my young hillwalking friends Roddy Woomble and Gareth Russel, both members of the rock band Idlewild, once played a gig in the village hall and were horrified to see their audience was made up virtually exclusively of semi-drunk fishermen, all clad in yellow oilskins and clutching six-packs of Tennent's lager. It was apparently the scariest gig of their career!

Time to think about the journey ahead and enjoy a quiet moment before leaving Lochinver.

SETTING OUT

There wasn't an oilskin-clad fisherman to be seen as my wife Gina and I left our car in the car park next to the petrol station and I jotted down a note to put through the letterbox of the police office across the road. I said we'd be leaving the car for a few days, left my mobile number and said when we'd be back to reclaim the car. The last thing I wanted was for the local cop to assume I'd wandered in towards Suilven and had an accident, leaving my car unattended in Lochinver. I also hoped that my faith in the nation's constabulary meant that he'd keep an eye on it for me!

A signposted turning, off Lochinver's main street a little south of the Assynt Visitor Centre, leads to a single-track tarred road that runs some three kilometres to Glencanisp Lodge, nestling in its Victorian splendour on the north shore of Loch Druim Suardalain. The start of the Sutherland Trail eases you gently into this rough and tumbled country where the Lewisian Gneiss, the bones of the land, pierces the thin-soiled skin.

Where the tarmac stops, a bulldozed track begins, used mainly by estate argocats and walkers, taking you behind the flaking Lodge, which is now run by the Assynt Foundation. This rambling building was once the showpiece of the Glencanisp and Drumrunie Estate, which was bought by the Assynt Foundation in 2005. The Lodge is being renovated with the help of Lottery funding, and it's to be hoped that this will help the Foundation make more profitable use of it in the future.

Glencanisp Lodge, once owned by the Vestey family, is now under the guardianship of the Assynt Foundation, who have recently received financial help to redevelop the building.

The track runs east for five kilometres to the bothy at Suileag, a glorious walk that runs high above the Abhainn Bad na h-Achlaise, a broad burn that flows down from the heights of the Glencanisp Forest, through a series of small lochans, to Loch Druim Suardalain. Banks of yellow broom and tall bracken grow on each side of the track and even this early on in the walk Suilven held our attention – commanding, imposing and totally dominating everything else in the landscape.

There's something about this hill's shape and character than has given it an almost legendary status and it stands out as one of the most impressively shaped mountains in Scotland. Go to the beach at Achnahaird and take a look at the profusion of mountains that rise from the horizon. Ben More Coigach, Stac Pollaidh, Cul Mor and Cul Beag, Canisp and Quinag, and there, in the middle of them, catching the eye as few other mountains do, lies Suilven.

Rising from the sodden moorlands of Inverpollaidh and Assynt, Suilven stands in isolated splendour, and that's one of the factors that makes this region of north-west Scotland so visually stunning. I've heard many hillgoers swear that the landscape north of Ullapool is God's own country, and there is nowhere else quite like it in the whole of Europe. When rain curtains sweep across the knolls and tumbled moors of Inverpollaidh, and the dark clouds are pierced by shafts of brilliant light, then Suilven boasts to the world why she has iconic status amongst Scotland's marvellous mountains. This mountain is certainly special.

" Banks of yellow broom and tall bracken grow on each side of the track … "

CROFTING AND COMMUNITY

Although not directly affected, Suilven became the symbol of land reform in Scotland in the 1990s. In February 1993, the Assynt crofters, after a long fight, finally purchased the North Lochinver Estate, where their families had crofted for generations. A very fine book about the buy-out, *We Have Won the Land*, by John MacAskill, has an image of one of the crofters, Allan MacRae, standing on a rock, arms raised, with a bottle of champagne in one hand and his sheepdog at his feet. Beyond him soar the vertical ramparts of Suilven.

Suilven, with Loch Veyatie in front, viewed from Cul Mor.
A somewhat neglected hill, Cul Mor offers panoramic views of the surrounding countryside.

It's difficult for non-crofting folk to fully comprehend the emotions that were felt in Assynt when the long, drawn-out negotiations finally came to an end and the Assynt crofters became the owners and custodians of the land on which they lived and worked. Many of the current generations are descendants of those who had been cleared from the more fertile hinterland to the coastal fringes during the Highland Clearances and they have a very direct connection with the land. John MacKenzie was one of the directors of the Assynt Crofters' Trust and when I interviewed him on the foreshore beside his croft at Culkein Drumbeg he paused when I asked him how the crofters felt when the news came through that their offer had been accepted.

John gazed at the ground for a moment, and when he raised his head a single tear ran down his face. He swallowed deeply, took a deep breath and told me, quietly and firmly, that he wished his grandfather had been there when the news arrived. His grandfather, who had been displaced from Inchnadamph to this very coastline, to this very croft where he had cleared the land of rocks and boulders with his bare hands to create tiny fields in which he could grow some crops, would have been immensely proud. John told me that the realisation of what the crofters had achieved took a long time to sink in. It was, in fact, a ground-breaking moment in the recent history of the Scottish Highlands.

> **❝ John told me that the realisation of what the crofters had achieved took a long time to sink in. ❞**

John MacKenzie of the Assynt Crofters' Trust who, on 1st February 1993, made history with Scotland's first community land buy-out.

At the age of 16, James Morrison is a child of land reform in the Highlands. He told me of his pride in working his own croft that lies a stone's throw from John MacKenzie's place at Culkein Drumbeg.

"I can't see myself doing anything else," he told me. "I love to work outside, I don't want to move away, and this is my home."

James may not be typical of young folk of his age but I wonder if the pride and determination of the Assynt crofters has rubbed off on him, if the knowledge that he is working his own land, and not a rented croft, and that he has security of tenure, has encouraged him to make a career from crofting.

"This place needs crofts and crofters," he said, waving his arms over the pastures and shoreline behind him. "Without the sheep and the cattle the place would become overgrown with rank scrub and would look completely different." If he could ask Scotland's First Minister for one thing, what would that be, I asked him. He replied: "Cut down on the bureaucracy that is tied to crofting. Someone once described this lifestyle as looking after an area of land that's completely tied up in legislation. It would be great if there was a lot less bureaucracy and more help from the government to help young crofters like me."

In 2005, some years after the success of the Assynt crofters, the residents of Lochinver and the surrounding area bought the Glencanisp and Drumrunie Estate from the Vestey family, under the provisions of the *Land Reform (Scotland) Act 2003*. The area, 18,000 hectares of stunningly beautiful land, includes some magnificent mountains as well as Glencanisp Lodge, and an awe-inspiring, wildlife-rich world of lochans, rivers and hills. The Assynt Foundation, not to be confused with the Assynt Crofters' Trust, was born.

This form of community land ownership isn't generally considered as an end in itself, but as a means of obtaining wider economic and social development, particularly within the Highlands and Islands area. Fundamentally, the buy-outs have given local folk a say in the management of their own land, and the spirit of land reform could be described as an act of liberation, giving the people an opportunity to take more command of their own lives and, ultimately, their own destiny.

It won't be easy, that's for sure, and already both the Assynt Crofters' Trust and the Assynt Foundation have faced some difficulties and internal turmoil. Dr James Hunter is a former chair of the Crofters Commission and Highlands and Islands Enterprise, and for him, land reform is "one of the keys to ensuring, in the Highlands and Islands especially, that the Scottish Parliament takes the steps needed to make Scotland a better, freer, place."

SUILVEN – THE AESTHETE'S MOUNTAIN

Gina and I stopped for a break at the two-roomed bothy at Suileag and here, sitting in the late afternoon sun on the old wooden bench by the wall, it was hard to imagine a more scenic place to live. But you can't eat scenery, you can't feed your children on fresh air and pretty views. We thought of those who had lived here in this small cottage, crofters perhaps like John MacKenzie, but unlike John, crofters who had been forced to move away because of economic uncertainty or failing crops. The former inhabitants of Suileag might well have been cleared from the land like thousands of others, forced away from their homes to an uncertain future. If you believe in such a thing as a 'spirit of place', as I do, then it's not surprising that an air of sadness still haunts these remote places.

*The last of the evening light illuminates Scourie Bay with
the crofting township and Ben Stack in the distance.*

66 *... it's not surprising that an air of sadness
still haunts these remote places.* **99**

We didn't linger long at Suileag – the sun was shining from a blue sky, the trail ahead was beckoning, and Suilven had changed its shape and colour again. The steep barrel-like ramparts of Caisteal Liath had now morphed into something less imposing but no less grand – the rounded summit eased off eastwards to the high Bealach Mor, beyond which the ridge appeared spiked and jagged. Ahead of us the western prow of Canisp, a greatly underrated mountain, loomed above the rocky knolls and hollows of the moorland. The waters of Loch na Gainimh lay like quicksilver in the hollow between the two hills.

It would have been tempting to simply roll our sleeping bags out on the floor of the bothy, cook an early supper and settle in, but we wanted to climb Suilven in the evening and spend the night in our tent by Loch na Gainimh. Reluctantly, we returned to the main path, crossed the burn by a bridge and, by a small cairn at the side of the track, set off up the steep and muddy footpath that climbs to the Bealach Mor of Suilven.

We had dumped our packs close by Loch na Barrack so it was a relatively easy climb, despite the eroded, crumbling path. The summit path, beyond the curious wall, wound its way up and over a couple of subsidiary tops before levelling off on the broad summit dome.

Under way at last, and with 120 kilometres of walking ahead, Cameron approaches the summit of Suilven at the start of the Sutherland Trail.

Aesthetically this was the start of our Sutherland Trail. Beyond the steep spires of the hill's eastern summits we could trace our route beyond Lochan Fada and over the shoulder of Canisp before dropping down to Inchnadamph. Sitting here, backs against the big summit cairn, gazing out across to Stac Pollaidh, Cul Mor and Cul Beag rising from the lochan-splattered moorlands of Inverpollaidh, we both sensed that feeling of 'crossing over' that so often comes close to the beginning of a long walk, when the pressures of arranging the trip and travelling to the start begin to ease off and the worries about weather and pack weights and food drops and a thousand and one other things begin to slough off like snow melting from a dyke.

Relaxed and thrilled by the prospect of the days ahead we stood on the summit, hand in hand, and took in the view – west to the sea and out, beyond the horizon, to Tir nan Og, the fabled Land of the Ever Young, and then east to the route that revels in its northness, where the quality of the light is matched only by the sweetness of the air, a place that is far removed from the sobriquet that is often bestowed on Sutherland – that of the so-called Empty Lands.

Even now, at the early stage in the journey that was to become the Sutherland Trail, we began to doubt the accuracy of that description. We came off the hill in the gloaming as the sun dropped towards the horizon and we pitched our tent by the gently lapping waters of Loch na Gainimh. Behind us, Canisp turned red in the twilight and only the call of a black-throated diver broke the silence.

TO INCHNADAMPH

The short nights of a Highland summer are a backpacker's delight. Roused by the early morning sun shining on the tent, making it unbearably hot inside, we cooked and ate our breakfast by the loch's shingle beach. A warm breeze coming off the water was just sufficient to keep the midges at bay. As we ate we gazed at the mist drifting amongst the crags of Suilven, silvery wreaths of cloud that emphasised the gaunt relief of the buttresses and ridges, the skeleton of a mountain almost as old as time itself. We pondered these phenomenal geological timescales, well beyond our ken and our comprehension of the tens, if not hundreds or thousands of millions of years that it has taken to wear these hills into the familiar shapes that we have come to love and admire.

What immense forces have worked here, so slowly and so deliberately? Great tectonic plates, moving at a fingernail's distance a day, forces that have inexorably moved this land we call Scotland from a position somewhere near Antarctica, all the way up to what we know as Florida, then north-east to where we are today, conjoined in a geological embrace with the land mass that we now recognise as England. And in our comparatively minute life-spans we are unaware of such massive movement, such slow and deliberate migration that may even yet, in the millennia to come, thrust our land mass ever eastwards towards Scandinavia.

And it's not only the painfully slow movement of the great tectonic plates that shapes our landscapes but the endless scouring of winds and frosts, the freeze–thaw cycles of snow and ice and the glaciers that created these great glens. Even in these days of global warming, the complexities of climate patterns are such that we may even see the return of glaciers in Scotland as Arctic ice melts and affects the strength and direction of the Gulf Stream drift, robbing us of our mild maritime climate and replacing it with frigid, agonising cold.

Such thoughts were far from our minds as we packed up the tent, hoisted our packs on our backs, and set off south-east alongside the Allt a' Ghlinne Dorcha, climbing gently through a narrow defile between the lower slopes of Canisp and the steep-sided Meall a' Mhuthaich. Beyond the gorge lay the lapping waters of Lochan Fada, where the path crossed to the south shore and followed the indentations of the loch's bays and inlets before climbing above the loch, dominated now by the slopes of Canisp, whose eastern shoulder we would shortly traverse.

Lochan Fada is a beautiful loch, in a magnificent setting. Nestled below Canisp, its waters reflect the changing shapes and colours of Suilven. We sat above the waters of the loch and looked back in the direction we had come and gasped in astonishment at the transformation of this amazing mountain.

❝ What immense forces have worked here, so slowly and so deliberately? ❞

From the very start of the walk you are rewarded with exceptional views and these continue almost every step of the way. Canisp and Suilven flank the background, while Loch Druim Suardalain by Glencanisp Lodge dominates the foreground. A scene to enjoy before the hard work begins!

Meall Beag, Suilven's eastern prow, spired tall and aloof into a blue sky. It was hard to believe this was the same mountain we had gazed at from Lochinver, and we knew that its shape would change again as we climbed over Canisp and saw it from yet another perspective. We also knew that as we left the footpath that ran alongside the southern shores of Lochan Fada and gained some height on Canisp, the view across the watery moors would throw up those other giants of the region, Cul Mor and Cul Beag, the Pollux and Castor of Inverpollaidh, and the most unlikely shape of Stac Pollaidh, the little hill that is a mountain in every sense other than height.

We sat in the sun by a roaring waterfall and drank in the view, aware that we were leaving a remarkable landscape behind us. We had only walked through it for less than two days but already we felt part of it, embraced and beguiled by it, very much in love with it and now we were to spurn it, turning our backs on it. I think we were both momentarily saddened when, crossing over Canisp's broad shoulder, Suilven's momentous outline disappeared from view for the last time, but we both knew that is the nature of multi-day backpacking. On long routes from Morocco to the Himalayas, from the US to the Alps, we have crossed hundreds of divides that separate one type of landscape from another, one kind of memory from another, one kind of experience from another. Although we were saddened to leave the remarkable landscapes of Inverpollaidh and Assynt behind us, we knew that in front of us, rising from the green glen of the River Loanan, were the hills and mountains of Inchnadamph – the bold Conival and Ben More Assynt, and the long bold ridge of Breabag.

❝ *… we were leaving a remarkable landscape behind us.* ❞

From Cnoc Breac above Elphin, the waters of Loch Veyatie and Cam Loch,
the rolling moorland and summits of Suilven and Canisp combine to
produce an unmistakable Sutherland landscape.

Canisp – "forms a fine viewpoint"

And we musn't forget little Canisp. Although our route only took us over the shoulder of Canisp it would be wrong to dismiss this fine hill in only a couple of sentences. An old Scottish Mountaineering Club guidebook of the 1930s describes the 846 metre mountain as "uninteresting" and then relents slightly by suggesting: "as it is in the midst of so many striking and shapely hills it forms a fine viewpoint." Mmm … it's exactly because it is such a fine viewpoint that Canisp is anything but uninteresting!

In terms of ascent Canisp is simplicity itself. From the head of Loch Awe on the A837 Ullapool to Durness road, the hill rises in a long, slightly curving ramp to its summit whose slopes then fall precipitously on three sides. It's a long and steady pull from the road, initially over swampy, grassy ground, then over drier, shattered screes and slabs of Lewisian Gneiss. My recommendation is to keep well to the left of the ridge and enjoy the drama of the Inverpollaidh landscape as it unfolds below you.

As you climb higher, this low-lying landscape begins to open up and its topography becomes more and more astonishing. The bumps and hillocks and ridges are underscored and pock-marked by dozens of pools and lochans – and several long and linear lochs, angled in exact parallels, slash their watery course across the mottled landscape. On the far edge of this watery wilderness the spired peaks of Cul Mor dominate the curiously primeval outline of Stac Pollaidh and as you climb higher the fortress-like shape of Suilven dramatically appears out of the west.

As you climb over the bump of Meall Diamhain and onto the final summit slopes, your eyes will be led beyond Suilven, beyond

> **" As you climb higher, this low-lying landscape begins to open up and its topography becomes more and more astonishing. "**

the immediate coastline to the distant Trotternish ridge of Skye and beyond to the blue hills of Harris, shimmering on the far horizon. Further north, beyond the mass of peaks and ridges that is Quinag, lie the conical outline of Ben Stack and the snow-covered ridge of Arkle – hills of the Sutherland Trail we would be meeting in a few days' time.

LEAVING INVERPOLLAIDH

The sadness at leaving the Inverpollaidh landscapes didn't linger, and we were both surprised to find ourselves padding across vast slabs of sun-warmed rock, linking up as many as we could to avoid struggling through the deep heather. I had been a little concerned about this section of the route, the only section between Lochinver and Tongue that involved off-track walking, but in reality it was a pleasure, an easy climb from the eastern reach of Lochan Fada onto the ridge, an undulating traverse of Canisp's east-facing slopes and a steep, but straightforward, descent to the River Loanan just beyond Stronchrubie.

Photographers should remember to take plenty of memory cards or films and batteries. The trail provides almost limitless opportunities for creative camera work.

As we made our way down steep heather-covered flanks towards the river I recalled the theory of Colin Fletcher, a Welsh-American outdoors writer whose work has been a huge inspiration to me over more years than I care to remember. Colin thought up a cardinal rule of travel, which I believe is pertinent to everyone who goes backpacking. Essentially, Colin Fletcher claimed you can only come close to the land by walking on it – the less there is between you and the environment, the more you appreciate that environment. It's obvious that you'll feel closer to the land by walking over it than travelling through it in an air-conditioned, 50-seater coach! It's the same in sailing – a solo yachtsman learns more about the sea than a passenger on the QE2, and indeed, someone bobbing about like a cork in a sea kayak will feel closer to the sea than someone in a yacht, experiencing more of the moods of the ocean, and the winds and the stars at night.

But Fletcher's law has a second and less obvious application – your appreciation varies not only according to what you travel 'in' but also according to what you travel 'over'. Drive along a motorway in any kind of car and your contact with the land is zero – you might as well be watching a television screen as the countryside whizzes past at 70 miles an hour, but turn off the motorway onto a country road, open the car window, and you come a tad closer to connecting with the land.

A narrow country road is better still, but it's then that you discover a corollary to Fletcher's law: "The further you move away from any impediment of appreciation, the better it is." By walking along a track you begin to appreciate the detail that turns a pretty countryside into a living, vibrant landscape – but leave that track for a faint footpath and you come even closer to the feel of the land. Almost inevitably, once you leave the footpath for an open hillside, completely devoid of any sign of man, you bring other senses into play – you can smell the crushed bog myrtle beneath your feet and your attention is taken up with the ground immediately in front of you. And it's then, and probably only then, that you can begin to feel at one with the land.

> **"** *… you can only come close to the land by walking on it – the less there is between you and the environment, the more you appreciate that environment.* **"**

On the 130 kilometres of the Sutherland Trail there are countless opportunities to apply Fletcher's law and connect with the environment.

Totally at one with our surroundings now, only the heat was a discomfort. Once off the hill the river was easy enough to cross – weeks of dry spring weather had reduced the water levels to a mere trickle, and we followed the gorse-clad banks of the river all the way to Inchnadamph, delighted that we didn't have to walk along the busy A837 road. I suggested to Gina that it might be nice to stop at the Inchnadamph Hotel for a beer. We could then push on a bit in the cool of the evening and find a spot to pitch the tent.

When we reached the old hotel, where the intrepid geologists Peach and Horne regularly stayed, I stopped outside to try and find my wallet which was somewhere in the depths of my pack. Gina went inside to see if the bar was open. When she came back outside she had a look of triumph on her face.

"There is a bar, and it's open," she told me before adding, "and they also have a bedroom that I've just booked for the night. I need a cool shower and a soft bed. You can go and camp if you like!"

There was something of an ultimatum in her voice, and I've been married to her long enough to know not to argue. A night in the hotel it was …

INCHNADAMPH TO LONE

The village of Kylesku is dominated by the distinctive ridge of Quinag and its three summits of Spidean Còinich, Sàil Gharbh and Sàil Gorm.

I don't know how many times I've passed the sign to the Bone Caves. It's prominent enough, by the side of the A837 Inchnadamph to Ullapool road, about four kilometres south of Inchnadamph, but I guess my mind is always on other things when I'm in these northern parts. With peaks like the Coigach giants on your immediate radar it's tempting to ignore some holes in the ground.

Holes in the ground? The 19th century geologists Benjamin Peach and John Horne would probably turn in their graves at that description, for it was this pair who first excavated the Creag nan Uamh caves in 1889, finding the bones of animals that were thought to have inhabited this part of Scotland during the last Ice Age, some 11,000 years ago.

After Peach and Horne's initial excavations of the Bone Cave, the Reindeer Cave and Badger Cave were explored and named in 1926. Animal and human remains have been discovered, suggesting that man had populated northern Scotland very soon after the last ice sheets had melted, some 10,000 years ago.

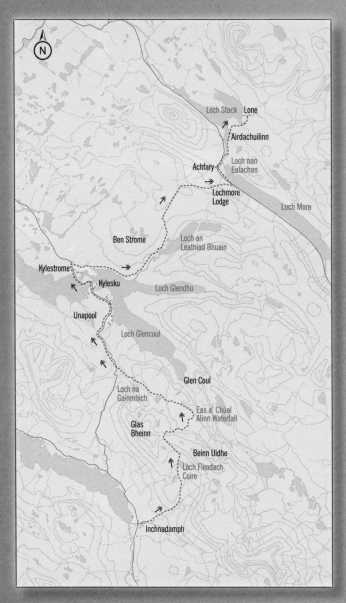

Inchnadamph to Lone

Map
Ordnance Survey 1:50,000 Sheet 15
(Loch Assynt); Sheet 9 (Cape Wrath)

Distance
40 kilometres / 24 miles

Approx. time
2 days

Terrain
A combination of good stalkers' paths, some road walking and bulldozed hill tracks.

Route
Leave Inchnadamph on the track that runs up Gleann Dubh but after one kilometre look out for a cairn at the side of the track. This heralds the beginning of a stalkers' path that climbs uphill beside the Allt Poll an Droighinn and continues N by Loch Fleodach Coire before climbing over the high bealach between Glas Bheinn and Beinn Uidhe. Cross the bealach and continue on the path as it descends in zig-zags towards the Eas a' Chùal Aluinn waterfall. Take the diversion to the waterfall then return to the main path, follow it through the Bealach a' Bhùirich and down to Loch na Gainmhich. Follow the road to Kylesku.

Leave Kylesku, cross the bridge over Loch a' Chàirn Bhàin, and follow the road for 1.5 kilometres to Kylestrome. Turn right off the main road, go through a gate signposted as the Reay Estate and follow the road past the buildings. Continue towards the old pier but as you approach it turn left onto a track and follow this along the shore all the way to a path junction above the Maldie Burn. Turn left at this junction and follow the track for 5 kilometres to another path junction. Turn right, follow the path over the Bealach nam Fiann and descend to Lochmore Lodge. Turn left onto the main road and follow it past Achfary for 2 kilometres, then turn right onto another track, cross a bridge over the river, turn left and follow this track past Airdachuilinn to the locked building at Lone.

Accommodation
Kylesku Hotel: 01971 502231;
www.kyleskuhotel.co.uk.
Friendly staff, fabulous food, local ales, sensational location. Reasonably priced and highly recommended.

No accommodation at Lone but plenty of good camping spots near the locked building.

Illuminated by a patch of sunlight, the Moine Thrust can be seen clearly rising from right to left at the side of Loch Glendhu.

Peach and Horne (the pair are synonymous with each other, like Morecambe and Wise or Little and Large) worked together for 40 years, and first explored the north-west Highlands, the scene of their most famous work, in 1883. They had been sent north by Professor Archibald Geikie, at that time Director of the Geological Survey, to try and resolve a long-standing controversy about the geological structure of the area. Geickie had long sided with the views of his predecessor, Roderick Murchison, who believed the fossiliferous Cambro-Ordovician Durness Limestone passed conformably upwards into the Eastern Schists of which a large part of the northern Highlands are formed. However, some geologists, particularly Charles Lapworth and Charles Callaway, believed that the metamorphosed schists must be older than the unmetamorphosed limestones below them, and that the junction was a steep fault. Since it could easily be demonstrated in the field that the junction is almost horizontal, Murchison's views were generally held to be correct. However, in 1883 Callaway and Lapworth suggested that the junction was a low-angle tectonic thrust, and this idea was given serious consideration by Geikie.

It was during their first season of field mapping in the region round Durness and Loch Eriboll that Peach and Horne recorded the true situation. Instead of the simple conformity that Murchison had suggested, there were gigantic structures of a kind never before encountered in Britain. The Eastern (Moine) Schists had been thrust westwards by a series of large-scale low-angled faults over the rocks of ancient Lewisian Gneiss and their cover of Torridonian sandstone and limestones. During this process a series of smaller faults had been produced in the underlying rocks. The thrust zone, now known as the Moine Thrust, was eventually traced in the field, all the way from Loch Eriboll to Skye. These well-exposed structures now seem easily recognisable, but it was perhaps one of the most spectacular discoveries in British geology. By 1884 Murchison's views had to be abandoned in view of the rapidly accumulating evidence against them.

EXPLORING THE BONE CAVES

The Bone Caves are not on the exact route of the Sutherland Trail, lying about four kilometres south of Inchnadamph, fairly close to the foot of Canisp, but are certainly worth a visit. A good footpath runs east up to the caves from the car park beside the A837, following the waters of the Allt nan Uamh. Halfway up, if you're observant, you'll notice the stream suddenly appears from a large pool at a spot called Fuaran Allt nan Uamh ('Fuaran' translates as 'spring'). Beyond it the stream vanishes. In fact, you're walking through a geological structure of porous Durness dolomitic limestone, which exists to a depth sufficient for subterranean drainage. The caves, which can be seen at the foot of the cliffs ahead, are the ancient remains of subterranean water channels.

Higher up the path a branch goes off to the right but ignore it — you'll return that way later, but for the moment continue on the north bank of the stream (which can be a dry stream bed in times of low rainfall) below the rocky ramparts of Creag nan Uamh. Sit down for a while, make yourself comfortable, pour yourself a hot drink from your flask and allow your imagination to have free rein.

High on the crags above you, three cave entrances are quite prominent. These are the Bone Caves, and they help paint a picture of what life would have been like here between the major glaciation periods.

About 25,000 years ago, in the Late Devensian period, the whole of north-west Scotland would have been covered in ice. Reindeer antlers found in one of the caves are reckoned to be 24,000 years old, while bones of species now extinct in Scotland, such as polar bears, brown bears, lynx, lemmings and Arctic fox, have been found. There has also been evidence of habitation by Upper Paleolithic Man, who probably lived here between 40,000 and 10,000 years ago, in caves and sometimes in wigwam-type tents.

Time to visit the caves now – continue on the path, cross the stream bed and climb up towards the end of the glen before the path turns back on itself just below the main crags. A couple of small caverns herald the Bone Caves themselves, a series of chambers and passages with obvious entrances. These are part of a much larger system of passages, the biggest in northern Scotland, which bore into the hillside for at least a kilometre south of the Uamh glen.

There are other caves in the area – in the glen of the River Traligill near the south slopes of Conival and in nearby Glen Oykel – but the Creag nan Uamh caves are the best known, and the most easily visited. As you peer into the darkness beyond the main entrances consider that these caves are thought to be in the region of 150,000 years old. Radiometric dating suggests that ice-free conditions with flowing ground water existed at the time. Geologists might well prove me wrong, but I could imagine a great glacier slowly grinding down the glen of the Allt nan Uamh, tearing away the hillside beside it and revealing the three underground watercourses as caves. Animals, and men, would later use these caverns for shelter.

As you wander down the hillside path to meet the outgoing route, think of those who have tramped these hills before you, not only the clansmen of old but further back, beyond the Vikings to the cavemen, when the Scottish Highlands would have been virtually unrecognisable, a cold and dramatic landscape where life was cheap, and short lived. The thought of it almost makes the midges seem bearable ...

INCHNADAMPH AND ITS MUNROS

Inchnadamph has little more than a hotel, a lodge that offers bed and breakfast and has an excellent bunkhouse and hostel, and a few scattered houses. It also has a long and varied history stretching back many thousands of years and was the heart of medieval Assynt. Fragments of an early Celtic cross suggest an early Christian presence here. The ancient castle and burial vault of the MacLeods of Assynt can also be seen here and remains of flourishing pre-Clearance settlements can be found in the glen of the River Traligill.

Inchnadamph also marks the start of the Munro-bagger's route to Conival and Ben More Assynt. As impetuous youths, a mate and I once drove from Glasgow to Inchnadamph to tackle Ben More Assynt and Conival during the short night of the summer solstice. The idea was simple enough. We'd arrive in time to get our heads down for a couple of hours and as the dim light of night gave way to day, about three in the morning, we'd tackle our hills, giving us all day to drive south to Glasgow again. Two days to climb two of the most northerly Munros in the land.

I don't recall all that much about the climb – we were dozy with sleep, midges feasted off us, and rain and low cloud completely obscured the views. The experience, perhaps unsurprisingly, tended to sour my attitude towards the Assynt hills and it was years before I went back. As is often the case, the second experience was more memorable than the first, which is a good reason for climbing all the Munros twice-over!

The usual route to the Munros passes the Traligill caves and makes its way up to a high pass between Beinn an Fhurain and Conival. From this col it's a straightforward climb up the broad northern ridge to Conival's summit. From there, a crest of broken quartzite blocks and boulders stretches east to Ben More Assynt's north top. Underfoot the going is rough and the quartzite can be very slippery when wet, but there is a wonderful sense of spaciousness with long views both north and south. The ridge narrows in places, sometimes quite dramatically, but there are no real technical problems.

Ben More Assynt and Conival are occasionally climbed from the south by the River Oykel approaches, though this circuit from Benmore Lodge is a long one. The south ridge of Conival has unavoidable scrambling. Eastern approaches are almost unheard of,

At 998 metres Ben More Assynt, with its two summits, is the highest mountain in Sutherland.
It's seen here from the west with Loch Assynt in the foreground.

being very long with some pretty serious river crossings. If you want a longer excursion it's possible to extend routes from Conival along the northern ridges over the contorted Beinn an Fhurain.

THE NORTH WEST HIGHLANDS GEOPARK

Geologically the mountains around Inchnadamph are predominantly made up of gneiss (which is not so nice when wet), on top of which sandstone tiers have been weathered by frost and wind. While Ben More Assynt and Conival perhaps lack the mountain architecture of their smaller neighbours such as Stac Pollaidh, Suilven and Quinag, the two Munros rise from a desolate and water-scarred landscape, and their shy and retiring nature is protected by the rough, naked miles of their approach. There is a prehistoric rawness in their appeal. Their geology is also more complex. The gneiss bedrock rises to a greater height than on their western neighbours and on Ben More Assynt it almost reaches the summit. Add the crystalline Moine Schists that are also found here, the white quartzite blocks and the limestone glen below and you begin to understand why this area has been described an "internationally acclaimed geological showpiece", and well worthy of its international Geopark status. This North West Highlands Geopark is one of 25 partners in the European Geopark Network.

From Inchnadamph the grey screes of Conival's upper tiers contrast starkly with the lush pastoral tones of Gleann Dubh below. The vibrant green indicates the predominance of limestone, the porous nature of which is responsible for the pot-holes and water courses and the well-known caves of Traligill and its disappearing river. The Norsemen called it Troll's Gill – the giant's ravine!

Before leaving Inchnadamph we met up with an old friend, Donald Fisher, who once worked as a geologist with Highland Council before heading south to work in south Wales. The pull of the Highlands proved too strong for Donald and he and his wife moved north again to Scourie on the Sutherland coast from where he works as a part-time guide at the Scottish Natural Heritage interpretive centre at Knockan Centre in Inverpollaidh.

Donald is one of the most enthusiastic geologists you'll hope to meet, and his enthusiasm is infectious. That's what makes him such a wonderful guide. I've never been all that hot on geology but when you walk through an area like Assynt, with all the amazing geological features around you, you can't help but wonder how it all began.

"Where you were on the top of Suilven," Donald explained, "the landscape that you would see is formed of raw, hard bedrock, a landscape that is about 2,900,000,000 years old. The rocks are so hard that they have completely dominated the way in which the land has developed."

My experience with geologists is that they tend to bandy about massive timescales like 2,900,000,000 years as though they were discussing what happened last year. I had to admit I couldn't get my head around such times, but could geologists?

"I'll let you into a secret," said Donald, "I personally can't either. I have a theory that no geologist really knows what a million years is like."

I appreciated Donald's honesty, but what was it that made this area of Scotland so special, so worthy of its international designation?

"We have here a special structure," Donald told me, "where rocks were dislocated by shearing, by compressional forces within the Earth's crust. Older rocks, from far away – that is, to the south-east near Inverness – were thrust, or pushed horizontally, toward, up and over, the younger rocks of Sutherland. This was known as the Moine Thrust and in the next few days you are in for a very special treat by walking through this area.

"You're going to take a walk over and along the zone of the Moine Thrust structure itself. You're going to go over these mountain ridges and from the tops you'll have the most fabulous view of a land surface 2,900,000,000 years old."

I couldn't wait. It had been good to see Donald again and we left him as he continued south to see to his visitors at Knockan. We set off in the opposite direction, to pay our respects to the nearby monument erected to the memory of Peach and Horne, and to continue on our own geological pilgrimage along the Sutherland Trail.

> **❝** *I have a theory that no geologist really knows what a million years is like.* **❞**

THE THREE SUMMITS OF QUINAG

A year earlier Gina and I had dropped down the length of Gleann Dubh the morning after we had completed one of the toughest days on the Cape Wrath Trail, which runs from Fort William to Scotland's most north-westerly point at Cape Wrath. We had camped high above the River Traligill, a midge-infested campsite that encouraged us to get up and away early. From Inchnadamph we followed the road north for a while before following a trail over the western shoulder of Glas Bheinn and down to Loch na Gainmhich, a route that offered marvellous views across to Quinag, one of my favourite hills in the area.

Today tourists visiting the monument to Peach and Horne, just north of Inchnadamph, may have little idea how controversial their theories were and the long battle they fought for their acceptance.

When seen from its eastern approach, snow-capped Quinag can look daunting but a steady line leads up unerringly to its southern summit, Spidean Còinich.

At 808 metres, Quinag is a Corbett. The mountain is actually more of a small mountain range, with a series of peaks that form a key feature in the extraordinary landscape of Sutherland.

Shaped like an elongated euro sign, with steep and inaccessible buttresses forming the ends of the two upper prongs, the mountain's saving grace, as far as walkers are concerned, is the lower prong, which fades out into a long and gentle ridge and offers easy access to the hill's backbone.

Unusually for a Corbett, Quinag boasts three summits – Sàil Ghorm, at 776 metres, is the highest point on the top prong of the euro; Sàil Gharbh, is the highest summit of the whole mountain at 808 metres, on the middle prong; and Spidean Còinich is at 764 metres on the southern one. It's this south top that is supposed to resemble the spout of a bucket, giving the hill the name 'Cuinneag' – Gaelic for a narrow-mouthed water stoup. Pronounce it 'coon-yak'.

Sutherland's big waterfall

This time, we were keen to take a different route to Loch na Gainmhich, one that would take us to the top of Britain's highest waterfall, the Eas a' Chùal Aluinn. Ben Nevis and the Eas a' Chùal Aluinn waterfall have two things in common. They both boast the title of 'highest' – Ben Nevis is the highest mountain in the UK and the Eas a' Chùal Aluinn is the highest waterfall – but neither are the best examples of their type.

The Ben is certainly a wonderful mountain but I can think of several others I'd place above it in terms of grandeur and spectacle and while the Eas a' Chùal Aluinn may be the tallest free-falling waterfall in Britain at a bit more than 200 metres, I can think of others that look much more dramatic. The Falls of Glomach in Kintail comes immediately to mind, as do the Steall Falls in upper Glen Nevis, and the Grey Mare's Tail that tumbles down the hill from Loch Skeen in the Moffat hills.

But perhaps I'm being a little unfair to Sutherland's big waterfall. I'd visited the falls a couple of times before and on both occasions the waterfall has been less than spectacular, the braided cataract no more than a dribble, thanks to some gloriously dry weather that is not untypical in Scotland's north-west in early summer.

The weather in Sutherland can change quickly with little warning.
In early spring a squall blows in across Lochs Glendhu and Glencoul.

There are those who would claim that the best vantage point to view the falls is from the head of Loch Glencoul, and during the summer months a cruise boat sails up the loch every day from Kylesku. But for the fit and able, it's infinitely more satisfying to hike up to the falls yourself, either from the well-worn track that climbs up from Loch na Gainmhich on the A894 Kylesku to Inchnadamph road or via a longer route from Inchnadamph, a dramatically wild walk that nevertheless follows good paths through some of the most spectacular landscapes in the Highlands.

We took the latter route, taking the good stalkers' path out of Gleann Dubh, leaving the glen opposite a footbridge over the Allt Poll an Droighinn. The path makes its way steadily into a high and wide mountain corrie that cradles two lochs, Loch Fleodach Coire and Loch Bealach na h-Uidhe. The route takes a long traversing line above the second of these lochs before crossing over the Bealach na h-Uidhe itself, a stony place with phenomenal views north and east to Arkle, Foinaven, Meal Horn, Meallan Liath Coire Mhic Dhughaill and Beinn Hee, the great hills of the north.

On the north side of the pass, the stalkers' path takes a devious, curving line, wriggling between small, sparkling lochans before reaching a junction of paths above the waterfall. Someone has scrawled 'To the Fall' on a large rock and a line of untidy cairns shows the way to the top of the Leitir Dhubh, the precipice over which the waters fall.

To see the falls properly you have to cross the stream cautiously just above the lip and walk a little way to grassy terraces that offer better views of the tresses of the falls themselves, but be careful. Some years ago a woman fell to her death here. Her husband, an insurance broker who had just doubled the value of her life policy, was tried for her murder but the case was found not proven (a uniquely Scottish verdict, which some folk say means "we think you did it but we can't prove it!"). Despite that, he committed suicide two years later. As you gaze down on the falls it's almost impossible to imagine that the course of the cascade is four times higher than Niagara!

DOWN THE ROAD TO KYLESKU

From the path junction below the falls, the route now climbs again in a north-west direction, past the spectacular Loch Bealach a'Bhùirich and down through the bealach of the same name to Loch na Gainmhich by the A894. Just before you follow the shoreline back to the road, take a quick peek down into the quartzite gorge at the north end of the loch. This waterfall, known locally as the Wailing Widow Fall, often looks just as dramatic as the Eas a' Chùal Aluinn and is, in its own way, just as hidden.

With the wild walking behind us for the day, we were faced with about six kilometres of road walking down to Kylesku. Road walking it may have been but we didn't become too despondent about it, for two very good reasons. This is one of the most scenic of road walks imaginable, with the soaring buttress of Quinag on one side and the hills of Loch Glencoul on the other, including a fabulous view of the Glencoul Thrust from Unapool – complete with an interpretive panel telling you all about it – and the most magnificent view up the length of Loch Glencoul to the distant Stack of Glencoul.

By the time we left the main road and took the little road to tiny Kylesku we were more than ready for a drink and a good meal. We knew we would get both here. The little whitewashed Kylesku Hotel, an old coaching inn dating from 1680, is situated by the slipway where the car ferry used to ply its trade across the waters to Kylestrome. With an excellent restaurant, friendly family bar and cosy residents' lounge, the hotel is the perfect place for a night of unadulterated luxury after three days of wilderness hiking. We had posted a package here with enough food to see us through the rest of the trip – we had also booked a night in the hotel.

Old Alfred Wainwright had stayed here when making one of his television programmes about walking in Scotland and, for all his faults, the old codger certainly appreciated a good view: "Anyone with an eye for impressive beauty will not regard time spent at Kylesku as wasted," he said. "Twin peaks of Quinag dominate an awe-inspiring picture of great contrasts, of glittering waters cradled in the arms of dark and sinister heights: the silence is profound and the loneliness almost fearful. I could spend a day here, just looking. Kylesku is a wonderful place."

The Kylesku Hotel and former ferry crossing. Prior to the opening of the new bridge, various passenger ferries operated from the early 1800s.

It is, and so is the hotel. Owned and managed by a young couple, Struan and Louise Lothian, both the restaurant and the bar have splendid views of the loch and the surrounding hills. The food is fabulous, with menus specialising in local game and seafood. Fresh langoustine, spineys, lobster, crab, scallops, haddock and mussels are available daily and are complemented by a wide selection of real ale, wines and malt whiskies. The rack of langoustine is a house speciality, and arrives with an encore of fresh salad, a dip and a bowl of freshly made chips! When Struan and I sat down to the challenge of his langoustine rack I had to admit to something of a phobia about shellfish. A few years after Gina and I were married we had a holiday in Brittany and went to a restaurant where we succumbed to the challenge of the local *fruits de mer*. When the meal arrived the shellfish was arrayed on a three-tier cake stand, topped by a huge crab, and apart from one or two mussels we had no idea how to eat the stuff. We did what we thought was our best but when the waiter arrived he was horrified. How could he take all that perfect shellfish back to the kitchen, he said in broken English. I thought he was going to cry …

That experience prevented us from even trying shellfish ever again, so to prevent further embarrassment I asked Struan to show me how to remove the shell from a langoustine and what part you eat! I was surprised how simple it was and I was even more delighted that my long-held phobia was well and truly shattered. I tucked in to those langoustines like Rick Stein – they were so full of fresh flavour that I didn't even use the dip. Along with a bottle of cooled Chardonnay we were in seventh heaven …

"Any fool can be miserable," is one of Cameron's favourite sayings. In the lounge bar of the Kylesku Hotel there's not much danger of that happening!

INTO THE REAY FOREST ESTATE

Next day dawned almost too soon and after a superb breakfast of scrambled egg and smoked salmon, a mountain of it, we were on our way again, across the slender, sensuous curve of the Kyelsku Bridge to Kylestrome and over the high sprawl of land to Achfary on the Lairg to Laxford Bridge road.

Because of the sea-loch indented nature of the West Highland landscape, links across various stretches of water have been vital to the transport infrastructure of the country. Before the Kylesku Bridge linked the 130-metre stretch of water between Kylesku and Kylestrome in 1984, a detour of about 200 kilometres was necessary – three to four hours of driving on largely single track roads – if the ferry wasn't running. The roll-on, roll-off car ferry only began operating in 1975. Before that a normal car ferry ran from between the wars and a passenger ferry from the early 19th century.

I'm certainly old enough to remember waiting in a queue of traffic in Kylesku as the old ferry plied back and forth across the narrow fiord. There used to be a petrol station here, with an ancient hand pump, but it seems that in those days life was less frenetic than it is now and people seemed content enough to linger and perhaps stretch the legs and wait their turn to board the ferry. The Kylesku Bridge, just like the Ballachulish and Skye Bridges, have aided and abetted our reluctance to wait for things, even a car ferry, and I can't help but think that something rather special has been lost. Having said that, most of the local folk regard the bridge as a godsend, indeed, a necessity, removing a significant restriction to tourism in the far north of Scotland.

I must confess I'm not normally a great admirer of man's handiwork amid such natural beauty but Arup's (the architect) design is completely at ease with the surroundings. Indeed the construction was designed to complement the natural beauty of the site, and won several design and construction awards when it was opened. A two minute walk from the hotel takes you through the woods to the bridge and as you cross over the waters of Loch Glendhu take a moment, as we did, to think of the dark secret that these waters once kept.

The Kylesku Bridge, which was opened in 1984, has been called a wonderful example of the bridge builders' art. Its long, sleek lines make a clear statement in the landscape, yet it seems in keeping with its surroundings.

During the last war the XIIth Submarine Flotilla trained here. This unit of X-craft miniature submarines trained around the waters of Kylesku before setting off for Norway where they attacked and crippled the infamous German battleship, Tirpitz. The submariners and divers spent time here training, and a memorial at the north end of the bridge remembers those 39 servicemen and the locals of the area as people who "knew so much and talked so little." The secret of the X-craft training never left these waters.

We had to endure another couple of kilometres or so on the road before we could leave it and make our way through a gate where a sign heartily welcomed walkers. This was the entry to the Reay Forest Estate, owned by the Duke of Westminster. We had walked this route the year before as part of the Cape Wrath Trail so we knew we were in for a delight. On that trip we had left Inchnadamph in the morning and it was the middle of the afternoon before we started out on the eleven kilometre walk to Achfary but we were so taken with this high and untamed landscape that we camped close to the high point, beside a small burn. It was an idyllic and memorable wild camp in a wonderfully remote setting.

In the year since that long walk, Gina has often reminded me that her favourite part of the Cape Wrath Trail route was alongside Loch Glendhu between Kylestrome and the Maldie Burn. With lungfuls of sea air and the views back across the waters to the multi-tops of Quinag we were accompanied by oystercatchers and sandpipers but we knew that once we had crossed the Bealach nam Fiann we would be leaving the sea lochs and the salt air behind us. The crossing of such divides is often a bitter-sweet affair – leaving behind a landscape that you have become comfortable in and connected to, and exchanging that for new vistas, different hills, further challenges. On this walk we were leaving the western seaboard and moving inland and the next day we would be on landlocked hills, including one of the finest in the land – Foinaven.

After a few easy-going kilometres we left the flat lochside path behind and began the climb up the track beside the Maldie Burn, enjoying its numerous waterfalls and cascades. At the foot of the burn is a half-buried hydro building and plans are afoot to upgrade this little hydro scheme with a buried power line running across the hills to the grid at Achfary. I hope it can be done sensitively. On a sultry and dry morning it was hard to believe that this little burn could generate enough power to supply electricity – the pools were dried up and the loch above it, Loch an Leathiad Bhuain, was very low.

> 66 *There is nothing more delicious on a hot day's walk than stripping off your boots and socks and plunging your feet into cold water.* 99

Step off the stalkers' path that goes north-east from Kylestrome, and the landscape seems elemental. This stream is one of many above Loch an Leathiad Bhuain in remote country on the way to Achfary.

A fisherman's hut lay by a bay with a small wooden pier angling its way out on the waters of the loch. There is nothing more delicious on a hot day's walk than stripping off your boots and socks and plunging your feet into cold water. Refreshed, we stretched out on the shore and enjoyed some lunch – oatcakes and cheese, our staple midday meal when backpacking. A gentle breeze wafted off the waters of the loch and cooled us, and kept the midges at bay – a wonderfully peaceful break.

The track we followed is used by the estate for sporting purposes, deer stalkers and fly fishermen, and as it rises above the waters of Loch an Leathiad Bhuain it offers magnificent views along the length of the loch to Loch na Creige Duibhe and the hills beyond. It took me some time to recognise what they were before I realised they were on the other side of the Lairg to Laxford Bridge road, hills that we would be passing in a couple of days' time. The highest of them is a Corbett with the curious name of Meallan Liath Coire Mhic Dhughaill – the grey rounded hill of the corrie of Dougal's son. I'd love to know the history of that name!

It wasn't long before we passed our campsite of the year before, tucked away behind a low hill with a gentle stream flowing past and below an ancient stone bridge. We had arrived there in early evening and no sooner than we had the tent up and the first brew on the boil than a noisy argocat appeared with a couple of tweed-clad fishermen aboard. It looked as though they were heading straight for us but when they were close enough to see the whites of our eyes they swerved the argocat around in a spray of mud and peat, gave us a cheery wave, and vanished in a cloud of diesel and child-like enthusiasm.

But it was my own reaction that was interesting. For a few moments I thought they were coming to ask us what we were doing – did we have permission to camp, didn't we know this was private property? Years of combative instincts rose to the surface, despite the fact that I was well and truly aware that recent legislation in Scotland made it perfectly legal for us to be exactly where we were and doing exactly what we were doing. The *Land Reform (Scotland) Act 2003* gave the public a right of access to all land and inland water, provided that right is enjoyed in a responsible way, and included within that piece of legislation is the public's right to camp wild. Despite that, it took me some time to relax and allow the peace and tranquillity of the wild camp site to ease off the tensions. I guess it'll be some time before those natural instincts, built up over a lifetime of hill wandering and access campaigning, evaporate completely ...

The high point of this traverse of the Reay Forest Estate at the Bealach nam Fiann is at a height of 400 metres, by the remains of some old stone buildings marked on the map as a shieling. I confess to a fascination for these old ruckles of stone and the 'spirit of place' they engender. Often I'm happy to sit among the stones, or the old walls, and think of

The shieling on the descent to Lochmore Lodge.

those who have used these temporary seasonal buildings – the shepherds grazing their flocks on upland pastures or the families of crofters who would come up to the higher places during the early summer when their livestock were grazing common land in the hills. This transhumance system of agriculture had generally fallen out of use by the end of the 18th century.

There are various accounts of life in the shielings, some that paint a grim picture of subsistence farming in real life-threatening situations but most, especially the rich legacy of Celtic song and folk tales, remember with at least some fondness the carefree days of youth – hunting moorhen, climbing the hills, flirting with the opposite sex … A Gaelic bard, Donnchach Bàn, once wrote:

> *An t-uisge glan 's an t-àile*
> *Th' air mullach nam beann àrda*
> *Chuidich iad gu fàs mi*
> *S e thug dhomh slàinte is fallaineachd.*

> The fresh water and aroma
> That was found in the hill-tops
> Helped to promote my stature
> And left me hale and hearty.

Despite Donnchach Bàn's enthusiasm for the hale and hearty life, there is no doubt conditions were harsh. The shielings were roughly built, being just walls of stone with temporary roofs of heather supported on raised poles. A hole in the roof at its highest point served to let out the smoke from a central hearth. The men folk would come up first, probably in early June, and make sure the buildings were in reasonable repair before bringing their families up, with their cattle and goats. High on the hill the beasts could enjoy the fresh grazings and avoid trampling the ripening crops in the open fields down in the glen.

At this time of the year the villages in the glen wouldn't have been particularly pleasant places. Midges and clegs would have been horrendous (as they still are) and with the melting of the winter's snows the whole area around a village would be a morass of mud, made worse by the trampling of those beasts that remained in the glen. Moving up to the shielings also helped to improve the nutrition of the animals, and prevented disease arising from continued grazing on depleted land. And I've no doubt the young folk would be happy to escape the constant lecturing of 'the meenister'. The shielings were probably used for about six to eight weeks before the approach of harvest and the impending cattle sales brought everyone back down to the glens again.

There is little doubt that before the introduction of large-scale sheep farming in the Highlands, the hills and mountains offered a much richer pasturage than is to be found today. Sheep, once labelled as 'hooved locusts' by conservationist John Muir, graze the vegetation down to ground level and their grazings have to be well-managed to prevent the complete destruction of the grass. The cattle and goats kept by the original Highland people grazed in a much less destructive way.

There have been a few explanations given as to why the old customs of taking the cattle and goats to higher ground during the summer months was abandoned and I guess the proliferation of sheep farming in the 18th and 19th centuries had as much to do with the end of the shielings as anything else. The old hill pastures, which had traditionally been available to all for common use, were turned into single-occupancy tenancies for the sheep farmers. The local villagers were often 'encouraged' to pack up and move closer to the coastline to make way for the flockmasters and their sheep. Although much of this re-settlement has gone down in the history books as the Highland Clearances, there is no doubt that much of the change was due to economic pressures with more entrepreneurial landowners looking for ways to gain better rents from their land and to the fact that young people were beginning to move away from their traditional lifestyles and look for work in the growing industries of the south. Needless to say, some landowners and their factors were rather over-enthusiastic about clearing families to the coast, or encouraging them to emigrate, especially those factors and agents who had been promised land for themselves, but we'll hear more of that later when we visit Strath Naver, the site of some of most vicious Clearances in the Highlands.

BEN STACK

I was keen to linger awhile by the shieling but Gina, as ever, wanted to keep moving, so I snatched a couple of photographs of her beginning her descent with the promise of the days to come as a background – the big hills of Arkle and Foinaven. The other hill that filled the frame was one that can be seen from many points in Sutherland because of its sharp, conical shape – Ben Stack.

The year before, we had put Ben Stack on our itinerary for the Cape Wrath Trail. However, by the time we had reach the Bealach nam Fiann we reckoned that if we pushed it a bit we could reach our B&B near Rhichonich by tea-time. With thoughts of a good meal at the Old Schoolhouse, and maybe a couple of beers, all our good intentions of climbing Ben Stack were abandoned, but as Gina hadn't ever climbed it we did promise ourselves that we would return later in the year.

Shaped exactly as every child imagines a mountain to look. The iconic shape of Ben Stack seen from north of Scourie.

In the relative gloom of early winter we returned, approaching the watery wilderness of the Reay Forest from Lairg along the empty miles beside Loch Shin where man-made islands are used as nesting platforms by black-throated divers. Water run-off from the surroundings hills, due to overgrazing and forestry, has increased considerably in recent years and the traditional nesting islands often flood. The artificial islands rise and fall with the water level. Breeding levels have been successful and the bird's melancholy call seems to embody the spirit of these northern parts. The great Highland writer Seton Gordon once described the wild and compelling cry of the black-throated diver as one that might come from "one of the uruisgean or gruagachan which in tradition and folk-lore people those sea-girt isles." It's an eerie sound in the half-light of a late summer evening, especially if you're camped by some remote hill-loch.

At 719 metres, Ben Stack falls short of Corbett height but we had nevertheless admired it often enough – a rocky, conical and isolated peak that rises from the shores of Loch Stack in two steep bands of cliff-line. Its blunt, western nose is steep too, but beyond its roof-like summit ridge its south-eastern slopes fall away in a gentle and rounded ridge, the Leathad na Stioma. Footpaths curve their way round the west and south of the hill and the A838 hugs the shoreline of Loch Stack below its western cliffs offering alternative circular routes. We decided to tackle the steep west-facing nose first, before ambling down the Leathad na Stioma ridge with the wind at our back, returning to the car along the quiet road.

A well-maintained stalkers' path zig-zags its way from the road up to Loch na Seilge and from there it was simply a matter of getting the head down and plodding upwards through the rocky outcrops to the summit ridge. Mist spoiled the chance of far-flung views but created a micro-world for us to climb through, a dark world of exaggerated form where distance, height and steepness always felt out of context, and no more so than on the knife-edge summit ridge.

" … the bird's melancholy call seems to embody the spirit of these northern parts. "

In good visibility this would be no more than a pleasant amble, but in the wind and thick mist it felt exposed and dangerous. A sudden thinning of the mist put things in better perspective and made us feel a little silly – the tightrope ridge was no more than a narrow rib with flat turf below. The summit cairn was directly in front of us and a hundred metres beyond lay the trig point and what looked like a television mast!

The descent was kinder to us in terms of views – out along Loch More and Loch Shin and the wonderfully named Meallan Liath Coire Mhic Dhughaill and north to Arkle, Meall Horn and Fionaven.

Although only 719 metres high, an ascent of Ben Stack is exhilarating, especially from the west where the route leads straight to the summit. And on a clear day the effort is amply rewarded with superb views in all directions. This is looking north-west along the A838 and out towards Loch Laxford and Rhiconich.

For walkers on the Sutherland Trail, the easiest ascent of Ben Stack follows another route. From the Bealach nam Fiann a rough track runs in a north-west direction to the summit of Ben Dreavie where you can easily descend to another estate track that climbs up Strath Stack from Achfary before heading north-east to climb over Ben Stack's north-west ridge. The high point of this track, close to Loch Eileanach, gives access to the steep west ridge of Ben Stack. It's then a steep pull to the summit. The descent can follow the route described above down the Leathad na Stioma.

OSSIAN – AN 18TH CENTURY HOAX?

Leaning against the old stone walls of the shieling at the Bealach nan Fiann, I considered the name of this high pass. Could there be a link between this high pass and the Fianna warriors, the legendary battle troops of Fionn MacCumhail? Only a couple of weeks before I had walked the length of Loch Ossian and wondered at the legacy of the name Ossian, the bardic warrior son of Fionn MacCumhail himself. Ossian's collected poems offer a hint of another world, a romantic and Teutonic struggle between the warriors of Fingal and the Norsemen. They make fascinating reading, but we don't even know for sure if those poems were the original work of Ossian, or entirely composed by an 18th century scholar by the name of James Macpherson.

Macpherson was born at Ruthven, outside Kingussie, in 1736, and later taught at the village school. In 1762 he created a literary sensation by publishing what he claimed was the translation of the *Poems of Ossian*. His work had a polarising reaction from the literati of the time: the sceptics, led by Dr Samuel Johnson, hounded him remorselessly, yet ultimately his book was undoubtedly the forerunner of Romantic British literature as championed by such worthies as Blake, Wordsworth, Coleridge, Keats and Shelley. The work was particularly highly thought of on the Continent, possibly due to the strong Germanic quality of the poems, and it's said that Napoleon always carried a French translation in his pocket.

I'm fortunate enough to have a copy of the book, and I'm occasionally drawn to some of the poems, which have a particular resonance of the land and man's relationship to it. Indeed, it could be said that the *Poems of Ossian* performed a great service in drawing poets back to an understanding of man's kinship with the elements and the natural world. Many of the poems do indeed have an elemental quality – titanic imagery at its best:

> *Fathers of heroes, O Trenmor! High dweller of eddying winds! where the dark-red thunder marks the troubled clouds! Open thou thy stormy halls. Let the bards of old be near. Let them draw near, with songs and their half-viewless harps. No dweller of misty valley comes! No hunter unknown at his streams! It is the car-borne Oscar, from the fields of war ...*

Or, from the poem 'Lathmon':

> *Selma, thy halls are silent. There is no sound in the woods of Morven. The wave tumbles alone on the coast. The silent beam of the sun is on the field. The daughters of Morven come forth, like the bow of the shower; they look towards green Erin for the white sails of the King ...*

Ossian Macpherson, as he became known, died an extremely wealthy man, despite his critics, and his remains were taken to London and laid to rest in the Poets' Corner of Westminster Abbey.

To Achfary and Lone

With my head full of such romantic imagery (well suited in such amazing surroundings), I set off to follow Gina downhill. The descent from the Bealach nam Fiann to the road near Achfary is a little over a couple of kilometres and follows a newish bulldozed track, a descent whose awkward conditions underfoot are more than compensated by the views towards Britain's most northerly mountains – until you enter the trees, that is.

I caught up with Gina in the forest. She had decided to stop for a bite to eat in the shade but the midges had moved her on. From somewhere on the high crags to our right we could hear the call of young peregrine falcons but, search as I did through the mini-binoculars that I always carry, I couldn't spot the eyrie. The parents were obviously staying out of view, at least until we vanished from their sight!

The Sutherland Trail wends from the bottom left of this picture down to Lochmore Lodge, before passing through the centre by Loch Stack and Lone Bothy. It then continues in the far distance through Srath Luib na Seilich to eventually arrive at Gobernuisgach Lodge.

The Achfary Forest runs down to the road and protects the big house, Lochmore Lodge, from the western breezes. We went through a gate, then past a farmyard before another gate brought us to the A838 Lairg to Laxford Bridge road, our last stretch of tarmac before Strath More below Ben Hope. From Loch More and Loch nan Ealachan came the eerie calls of black-throated divers and above us a buzzard mewed in raptor response. We settled down into a steady rhythmic plod, our normal technique for coping with tarmac-bashing, even if it was, in this case, only for a couple of kilometres. I must confess that I'm not very keen on walking on roads – I have an arthritic left foot, which doesn't cope well with hard surfaces. It always feels as though the foot overheats when the ground is particularly unyielding, like tarmac or hard gravel tracks, and a certain amount of swelling takes place along the bottom of my toes. It's most uncomfortable but the pain eases off pretty quickly if I can submerge the whole foot in cold water, or even just take a break for five minutes, and that's what we did in Achfary village.

It's almost an exaggeration to refer to Achfary as a village. The settlement is part of the Reay Forest Estate owned by the Westminster family and was built to house families who worked on the vast sporting estate that stretches from Laxford Bridge in the west to Kinloch in the east. Most of the houses were built between 1853 and the 1870s. Today Achfary is probably best known for its unusual black and white telephone box, which was erected in the 1960s. Apparently, in these days of mobile phones, BT were quite keen to remove it but the Duke himself led a campaign to keep it in place, even though a spokesman for BT pointed out that only three chargeable calls were made from it in the whole of 2008. Apparently 26 free calls were made from it too …

The Reay Forest Estate offices used to be in a building close to the Village Hall but they have been moved to the top floor of a brand-new Steading Building, a two-storey office and workshed arrangement with its design based on the farmhouse previously occupying that spot. The front of the building contains a plaque that was first housed in the local church, which was later closed and the plaque moved to the farmhouse. Following the demolition of the farmhouse, which, at that time, was used as a workshop, it was decided that the new Steading Building should now contain this plaque. The plaque was originally erected by local people to the memory of the First Duke of Westminster who died in 1899:

> To express their deep regard for his character as a philanthropist at home and abroad, and for the courtesy and generosity exercised by him among them during his tenancy for about fifty years of the forests of Stack, Badnabay, Reay, Gobernuisgach, Ben Hee, Corrie Kinloch, and Glendhu, with the angling attached, he built lodges and dwellings, erected fences, made roads and paths … thus giving employment to tradesmen and labourers and adding to the comfort of many.

If you intend hiking the Sutherland Trail, or climbing any of the area's Corbetts during the stalking season, you can find out about stalking arrangements here in the Steading Building. There is also a post office in the village, but it's only open for one hour a day!

Shortly after leaving Achfary we crossed the footbridge over the stream that links Loch nan Ealachan and Loch Stack and made our way north on the track that leads past the keeper's picturesque house at Airdachuilinn. I've often passed this building and thought it one of the most marvellously situated houses in the Highlands. On the shores of Loch Stack, full of brown trout, it looks across the waters to Ben Stack and has the steep ramparts of Arkle towering over it. Not a bad place to spend your days, especially if you're into a bit of fly-fishing. I don't think I've ever passed Loch Stack without seeing at least a couple of rowing boats on the loch with anglers happily casting their rods. Much of the local economy is based on country sports such as shooting and fishing and while I don't think I could ever bring myself to aim a gun at a stag and want to kill it, I'm attracted by the guile and cunning and the knowledge of natural history that's involved in fly-fishing. We had planned to meet up with an old friend of mine, Bruce Sandison, one of Scotland's best-known advocates of angling and sport fishing, when we reached Tongue and I was looking forward to sharing a boat with Bruce for an afternoon.

Beyond the house the track skirts a peninsula jutting out into Loch Stack, crosses a couple of streams and goes over a new footbridge (the old one was washed away in a flood) over the Abhainn an Lòin, a river that we'd be following in a couple of days to cross the Bealach na Feithe and descend to Gobernuisgach Lodge and the historic Strath More, but for the moment we had to find a camping spot close to the old (locked) bothy of Lone.

> 66 … I'm attracted by the guile and cunning and
> the knowledge of natural history that's involved
> in fly-fishing. 99

I'm not sure I can recall a time when this so-called bothy was actually open to the public but I do know my old friend John Ridgway, whose internationally acclaimed School of Adventure lies up the coast at Ardmore, used to bring groups here on hillwalking trips. Indeed I think his daughter Rebecca, with whom I was delighted to make a television programme a number of years ago as part of my *Wilderness Walks* series for BBC2, uses it these days for groups from her Cape Adventures outdoor school, which she runs with her husband Will on the shores of Loch A'Chadh-Fi.

I must admit I've never been a big fan of bothies, so the padlock that firmly secured the cottage at Lone from wandering climbers or stravaigers didn't unduly worry me. As a young man I spent a number of years working in areas of deprivation in Glasgow and the smell of decay and the dank atmosphere of most bothies reminds me all too clearly of those inner-city experiences. Having said that, there have been a handful of occasions over the years when I've been glad to have a solid roof over my head when weather conditions have been too wild for a tent. One memorable night with my friends Liz and Simon Willis saw us camping close to Shenevall Bothy below An Teallach. In the course of the wee small hours a gale rose and one of the fierce gusts snapped the pole of my tent. Lying in my sleeping bag with the tent flapping around my ears like a demented banshee wasn't exactly conducive to sound sleep so I abandoned the tent in favour of a night with the mice of Shenavall. Liz and Simon slept through it all …

The locked bothy at Lone by the side of Loch Stack with Arkle framing the background.

A few short sentences in the Access Code that accompanies the *Land Reform (Scotland) Act* says it is perfectly lawful for backpackers to camp wild, provided they act responsibly. Older legislation once claimed it was against the law to form "an encampment" but that related to someone, or a group of people, setting up semi-permanent camps, like those of New Age travellers. Unfortunately, in the past, many land managers used that law to discourage wild, unobtrusive backpackers' bivouacs.

In general though, a blind eye is turned towards those who camp well away from roads and habitation, provided we leave no trace of our passing, and don't do any damage. Such wild camps can be extremely memorable and have been enjoyed by travellers since time immemorial. There is something very satisfying in being in such close contact with the natural world – to hear the call of an owl in the trees overhead, or waken to find a deer hind browsing quietly outside your tent, or to listen, still in bed, to the liquid warbling call of the curlew.

At such times the camper experiences an intense gratitude for such simple gifts. Such appreciation was beautifully articulated in *Travels with a Donkey* by Robert Louis Stevenson after spending a night under some pine trees in the hills of the Cevennes, in southern France. I like the sentiment behind the words, the idea of him paying his way:

> *I had been most hospitably received and punctually served in my green caravanserai. The room was airy, the water excellent, and the dawn had called me to a moment. I say nothing of the tapestries or the inimitable ceiling, nor yet of the view which I commanded from the windows: but I felt I was in someone's debt for all this liberal entertainment. And so it pleased me, in a half-laughing way, to leave pieces of money on the turf as I went along, until I had left enough for my night's lodgings.*

The late W. H. Murray, Scotland's finest ever mountain writer, was another enthusiastic advocate of the use of a tent when exploring remote quarters of the world:

> *To come suddenly on to a mountain plateau and there to see its lonely splash of fawn between silver snow and blue sky was in itself enough to lift a man's heart.*

That "splash of fawn" may have lifted Bill's heart, but his tent would have made modern backpackers grimace at the thought of carrying it:

> *The tent was made of reinforced cambric, fawn coloured, with sewn-in groundsheet, and at each end a circular sleeve-door and ventilator. A ventilator in use could either hang outside like a small wind-sock or be drawn inside – a point that proved of great importance. The poles were bamboo and the tent-pegs aluminium, broad bladed for snow. Around the outside ran a broad canvas skirt, on which snow or boulders could be piled up and the tent anchored independently of pegs. The guys were of stout rope. The tent's weight was ten pounds, and the size four feet high by seven feet long by four and a half feet broad. It was testified that the tent had withstood hurricanes of a hundred miles per hour in the Himalayas. The price was six pounds ten shillings.*

A modern backpackers' tent for two people, like the one Gina and I carried, weighs less than half of Bill's tent, although it costs considerably more. While good, reliable gear is important, I think I've realised over the years that the really vital point of wild country backpacking is that there can be an intense joy in simplicity. We live in a wonderfully complex world but occasionally that very complexity can create certain stresses and we long for a simpler existence, even if just for a short time. It's then that, tent up, ensconced in a sleeping bag and a mug of tea at hand, the tensions of life can begin to truly evaporate. The sheer simplicity of camping in wild places has been a way of life for nomadic tribes for thousands of years. Backpackers, like the early cavemen, revert to a hunter–gatherer status and life becomes simple again. And in that simplicity we also find restoration, rehabilitation and a certain amount of healing, a process that allows us to return to that other complex world and perhaps, just perhaps, begin to make some sense of it!

Piles of old rubble close to the river suggested the existence of former shielings and, after sniffing around for a while, we found a flat stretch of turf close to one of them, above some very attractive falls. With a backdrop of Arkle's steep south-west face and the footpath of the Sutherland Trail stretching out towards Srath Luib na Seilich in front of us we were well set up for the night. Tomorrow, all going well, we would camp high in the cradle of the area's three Corbetts – Arkle, Foinaven and Meall Horn. It would be good to get on some high ridges again, and enjoy a high-level camp among some of Sutherland's finest hills.

It's at this point that the Sutherland Trail walker has a choice of routes. The straightforward route simply travels east from Lone, up and into the Srath Luib na Seilich and over the 450 metre high Bealach na Fèithe, before descending gradually to Gobernuisgach Lodge and Strath More, a distance of about fourteen kilometres. Alternatively, a slightly higher-level route, and certainly a more mountainous one, follows another excellent path by the Allt Horn before curving north round Creagan Meall Horn and descending to Glen Golly and Gobernuisgach Lodge via the An Dubh Loch and Lochan Sgeireach. The path is clear and well constructed for much of the way but does become a little sketchy in the area around the An Dubh Loch. The highest point on this route is slightly over 500 metres so there's no big difference, in terms of being a good or bad weather alternative, to the Bealach na Fèithe route. What this higher route does offer though is access to Arkle, Meall Horn and Foinaven, so walkers who are keen to bag these three hills might find it easier camping somewhere close to the Bealach Horn below Foinaven's south ridge. The choice is yours.

❝ … in that simplicity we also find restoration, rehabilitation and a certain amount of healing … ❞

FOINAVEN

The long summit ridge of Foinaven from south-east to north-west dominates this view from the Kinlochbervie road.

I once had a curious conversation with a friend who had taken up hillwalking. He was thoroughly enjoying himself and reckoned his weekly hillwalking excursions had changed his perspective on life. He felt fitter than he had done for years, and felt more alert mentally, had less stress in his life, and he put it all down to his new hobby of climbing all the Corbetts – Corbett-bagging.

I was intrigued that he had taken up Corbett-bagging, as the vast majority of hillwalkers tend to start their bagging careers with the Munros, so I asked him why he had a preference for the Corbetts. He seemed surprised by my question. "Corbetts are smaller, and there are fewer of them," he replied, "so they must be easier."

Big mistake!

I suppose it's a logical assumption to consider the smaller hills easier to climb but most hillwalkers who have climbed both Munros and Corbetts would probably suggest the round of the Corbetts is more taxing, and takes longer than a round of the Munros. This is largely because the Corbetts are more strictly defined in terms of what constitutes a separate mountain in terms of re-ascent between adjacent hills, so the Corbetts are often much more distinct and separate hills than many of the Munros.

TRAIL INFORMATION

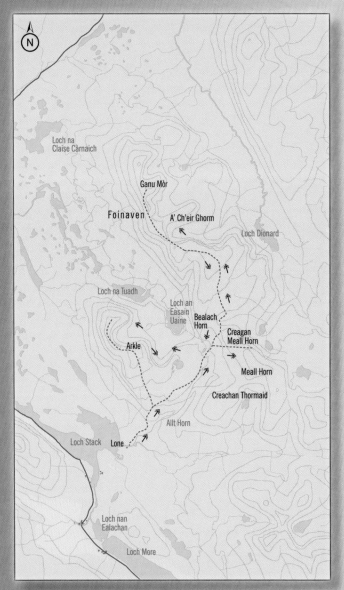

Foinaven

Map
Ordnance Survey 1:50,000 Sheet 9 (Cape Wrath)

Distance
24 kilometres / 15 miles

Approx. time
8–10 hours

Terrain
Hard mountain walking with some steep, loose rock conditions on the main Foinaven ridge.

Route
From Lone cottage take the path that follows the Allt Horn to the high bealach between Foinaven, Arkle and Meall Horn. Each of these three summits can be climbed from here. To climb Foinaven continue N to Creag Dionard, where a broad ridge runs in a NW direction to a spot height at 808m. From here the summit ridge runs roughly NW then N to Ganu Mòr, Foinaven's highest point (shown as 914 metres on the map, but re-surveyed in 2007 at 911 metres). From the summit return to the Bealach Horn where you have the option of climbing Arkle and Meall Horn before descending back to Lone.

Whereas you can often climb three or four Munros in one outing (you can climb seven on one route on the South Glen Shiel ridge), there are few Corbett groups where you can climb more than two or three on a single walk. That generally means Corbett days tend to be shorter days out, because you are mostly just climbing one hill, but it also means you need a lot more days out to get round them all.

I've never forgotten Munro guru Hamish Brown's advice. If you can, climb the Munros and the Corbetts together. There are many areas where great walks link both kinds of hill. It pays not to get too hung up on either Munros or Corbetts or any of the other lists, but to enjoy the hills as they come. At the end of the day it's the experience that matters rather than how many ticks you have in your guidebook. Having said that, there is little doubt that Munro-bagging, and indeed 'collecting' mountains of various heights, is as popular as ever.

Cameron striding out on the three kilometre summit ridge of Foinaven.

MOUNTAINS, LISTS AND TICKS

The completion of the world's fourteen 8,000 metre peaks is a rather more serious matter than climbing 284 Munros, or 221 Corbetts. The 8,000 metre height is entirely arbitrary of course, but roughly corresponds to the 'death zone' – the height at which the human body, even if kept warm and well fed, will never survive for more than a few days. The limited oxygen means that the body cannot function properly and gradually closes down. Combined with the cold, the terrain and the sheer physical and mental effort required, climbing any 8,000 metre peak presents a colossal challenge. The first 8,000 metre peak to be climbed was Annapurna in 1950, and within a decade, all fourteen had been climbed. And although some 3,000 mountaineers have stood on at least one 8,000 metre peak, the challenge these mountains pose is still immense.

And so, the world's 8,000 metre mountains remain the ultimate 'Mountain Collection'. Reinhold Messner was the first to make a solo ascent of Nanga Parbat and of Everest, and in 1986 became the first to climb all fourteen 8,000 metre peaks. He took sixteen years to complete his goal. According to him, the idea of climbing them all grew over time and was never the objective from an early stage. "I did not collect 8,000ers as has often been suggested," he wrote. In his early climbs, he seemed intent on pushing the boundaries – finding new routes, for example – on the great peaks rather than any notion of peak bagging. "I didn't feel especially heroic to have climbed all fourteen of the 8,000ers. I had seen something through, that was all," he wrote.

Alan Hinkes became the first Briton to complete all fourteen peaks when he climbed Kangchenjunga in 2005. Recognised as one of the world's top mountaineers, he once told me that when he completed the 8000ers he wanted to climb the Munros! Peak bagging must in his blood …

> 66 *… he once told me that when he completed the 8000ers he wanted to climb the Munros! Peak bagging must be in his blood …* 99

Climbing all the 4,000 metre peaks in the Alps has posed another challenge – Karl Blodig became the first to 'collect' all of these, completing his collection in 1911. In 1996, Scotland-based mountaineers and guides Martin Moran and Simon Jenkins became the first climbers to bag all the Alpine 4,000ers in one continuous expedition.

In the 1980s, the idea arose to 'collect' the highest peaks on all seven continents. In 1985 Dick Bass of the US, an inexperienced mountaineer and a multi-millionaire, became the first to complete this collection: Denali in North America, Aconcagua in South America, Everest in Asia, Elbrus in Europe, Kilimanjaro in Africa, Mount Vinson in Antarctica and Mount Kosciuszko in Australia. However, this list has been subject to many disputes, mainly about the inclusion of Australia. Australia can be considered to be in the continent of Oceania – which is why, in 1986, Canadian mountaineer Pat Morrow rejected Kosciuszko for the Cartensz Pyramid in Indonesia, the latter being over 2,000 metres higher than the former (and a considerably more demanding challenge). Reinhold Messner – who again argued that he was not 'collecting' mountains – and many others followed Morrow. Although a powerful symbol, the circuit requires comparatively little skill and experience. Everest, of course, is the great leveller but many Seven Summitteers nowadays hire guides to take them up Everest. The real challenge, some argue, is only time – and raising enough money.

The Munros is perhaps the world's oldest 'collection'. In 1890 Sir Hugh Munro compiled his list of the 3,000 foot mountains of Scotland, which were then collectively named the Munros. He would have little imagined that he was instigating a challenge and a tradition that a century later achieved the status of a cult. Reverend A. E. Robertson first completed the collection in 1901 and another 20 years went by before the achievement was repeated by another cleric, Reverend A. R. G. Burn in 1923. Perhaps church ministers only had to work on a Sunday and could spend the rest of the week climbing hills? Only eight people had completed the Munros before World War II. The first woman to complete the Munros was a Mrs J. Hirst in 1947.

If you think about it, Munro-bagging should have died out when the Ordnance Survey maps went metric – rendering obsolete the historic height of 3,000 feet – but quite the opposite happened. The list of Munroists now makes up a long line of statistics and records and 'firsts'– father and son records, people going solo, or in different seasons. Philip Tranter completed them a second time, leading to a row of multiple tallies; Hamish Brown did the Munros as a continuous walk in 1974 in 112 days and held the 'fastest ever' title for many years. This record was broken by Martin Moran who completed the 277 summits in 83 days, and managed to do so during the winter of 1984/5. (Occasional reclassifications of the list by the Scottish Mountaineering Club means that the total has varied up and down over the years, from 283 in Sir Hugh's original list to the 284 cited today.) My good hiking pal Chris Townsend became the first person to climb all Munros and Tops in one continuous expedition. The ages of the oldest and youngest have changed steadily; even dogs have topped all the magic summits!

So 'collecting' mountains is more than just setting a record – it's about setting your own challenge and achieving a personal dream, although some refuse to acknowledge their achievements as collections. Messner observed, "I am not proud of this 'collection' which I do not regard as such. I am not proud of the success, though I had sought it for a long time. But I am proud to have survived."

I completed my first round of the Munros in 1991, and the Corbetts a few years later. As I write I'm a handful of Munros short of my third round and yet I wouldn't describe myself as a Munro-bagger per se. I backpack, I ski-tour, I ride a mountain bike and occasionally still climb. Rarely a week goes by when I'm not in the hills, a habit that has lasted me almost 40 years, so I tend to 'pick up' hills as I go along and every so often I check what I've done against the Munro guide. Is this sort of 'mountain collection' an addiction? I guess it is, and a thoroughly delectable addiction it is too.

But what has all this mountain collecting got to do with the Sutherland Trail? Well, nothing really if you choose to stick with a low-level route between Lochinver and Tongue, but I suspect most hikers will be tempted into climbing at least one or two of the hills and if you're going to climb any of them then Foinaven should be high on your list of preferences.

FOINAVEN – MUNRO OR CORBETT?

In a sense Foinaven is symbolic. I, and many others, have often wondered how popular the hill would be if it was a few feet higher. At 2,988 feet it just falls short of Munro status and so escapes the trampling boots of Munro-baggers, but since it's one of the finest mountains in the northern Highlands, its height doesn't really matter. Most hillwalkers climb it because of its commanding position, because of its beauty and because it's part of one of the big hill days of Scotland – the traverse of its summit, along with its close neighbours, Arkle and Meall Horn.

Leading ever onwards – the final summit of Ganu Mòr is hidden from view.

In 1992 there was some concern among hillwalkers when a new survey measured the height of Foinaven as 914 metres, possibly elevating it to the status of a Munro. There were some fears this would make the hill the focus for a burgeoning army of Munro-baggers but eventually the Ordnance Survey settled on a height just under the magical 3,000 feet, and the tranquillity of Foinaven was assured, at least for a while.

I don't personally subscribe to the theory that our Munros are being trampled to death. Away from the busy hills the Munros are generally devoid of people and on most Scottish hills if I spot half a dozen people in a day then I regard it as busy. Scottish hills are still very much the domain of those who like to escape the crowds and Foinaven, because of its northern position, will never be a honeypot hill like Ben Nevis or Ben Lomond.

Continued speculation about the heights of the Ganu Mòr summit of Foinaven and Beinn Dearg in Torridon recently stimulated the Munro Society to commission surveyors to measure the mountains, using state-of-the-art GPS technology. The hills were last measured in 1992 and given a height of 914 metres. Unfortunately, the Munro height of 3,000 feet equates to 914.4 metres and the Ordnance Survey admits that their surveying methods of the time might not have been accurate enough to ascertain if the hills were above the 3,000 foot contour or not.

The arbiters of all things to do with Munros and Corbetts, the Scottish Mountaineering Club (publishers of the Munro's Tables since 1891), were reluctant to become involved in the debate, refusing to promote or demote any hill unless the change has been sanctioned by the Ordnance Survey. If the Munro Society's new measurements exceeded the magical 3,000 feet then it would be up to the Scottish Mountaineering Club to decide whether the hills should be promoted to Munro status.

As it happened, both hills failed to make the necessary height. In Foinaven's case, the surveyors discovered that the hill is even shorter than had been previously thought. The GPS technology used by the surveyors CMCR Ltd of Larbert, Stirlingshire, can measure heights to within plus or minus 30 millimetres. It was found that the hill fell short of Munro status by 12 feet (3.7 metres). The new height of the hill, which has since been ratified by the Ordnance Survey, has been given as 2,988 feet or 911 metres, three metres shorter than the last survey of 1992.

The view back south-east along Foinaven's long ridge. In summer it makes for a long day out;
in winter conditions, it is a major mountaineering expedition.

A spokesman for the Ordnance Survey later said that heights had previously been captured by aerial survey methods, whereas advanced computation methods were now being used. I wonder, now that such sophisticated equipment is available, if we could see more Munros demoted or Corbetts promoted? There are about a dozen Munros listed with heights between 914 and 918 metres and another dozen Corbetts between 914 and 911 metres, all falling within the margins found in the Foinaven result.

And for the dedicated mountain-bagger, a word of advice. There are two cairns on the Ganu Mòr summit of Foinaven. It's always been assumed that the eastern cairn was higher because the Ordnance Survey gave it a spot height of 914 metres and gave the western cairn a height of 911 metres, but in fact one of the climbers with the re-surveying group told me the western cairn is actually the higher of the two – the only way to make sure you've reached the highest point on Foinaven is to visit both cairns!

I must admit I felt a sense of relief when I was initially contacted by a reporter from a local radio station and told that Foinaven had failed to make Munro height. I'm sure many listeners sensed that relief too. It was rather curious, because I hadn't thought too much about it previously, thinking that if the hill did become a Munro then it would have been a bitter-sweet thing – great news for the local economy of Sutherland, but bad news in the sense that the hill might lose something of its peace and relative quietness. What really surprised me about the news was that Foinaven was a full three metres shorter than its last measurement. One can't help but wonder how many other hills are three metres shorter than their published height? And does it matter?

In all seriousness I don't think it matters a toss. Munro-bagging is only a game and the list-ticking only an excuse to travel all over the Highlands, climbing an extraordinary array of mountains. If the scientists are correct and global warming results in higher sea levels then we'll probably lose a few Munros anyway, depending on just how high those sea levels rise. The really important thing about the whole hillwalking game is not the height of the hills we climb but simply being out there, getting the exercise, enjoying the views, coping with the challenges of weather, underfoot conditions and navigation problems. The numbers game, the list-ticking game, is a side issue and I think that's why I breathed a sigh of relief when I heard that Foinaven had failed to measure up.

In spite of its obvious attraction – airy and with fine views every step of the way – we met only one other party when filming the television programme.

I rather like the fact that Foinaven will remain a Corbett. If I were to list hills in terms of their character and grandeur then Foinaven would most certainly be in my top 20. Perhaps we should see a new listing of Scottish hills. To quote Tina Turner, we should call them "Simply the Best", no matter what their height.

One newspaper report at the time of the re-survey suggested that naturalists and landowners would sigh with relief. The area around Foinaven is home to colonies of freshwater pearls, sea otters and rare waders, as well as scarce plants and bog habitats, and it is designated as both a Special Area of Conservation and a Site of Special Scientific Interest. Its remoteness, according to this particular broadsheet, has kept the mountain in near-pristine condition, a status threatened by "careless hillwalkers". I guess the reporter has never been on Foinaven. Parts of the main ridge are badly eroded, and at one point it's becoming dangerously eroded. But more of that later …

ARKLE AND MEALL HORN

In our riverside camp close to the old building at Lone we awoke to a cloudy, midge-infested morning. Breakfast was a hurried affair and we packed as much gear into our packs as we could before venturing out of the tent. Midge head-nets are a blessing in such conditions and the green netting hoods helped preserve our sanity and patience. I guess we were breakfasted, packed up and on the move within an hour of waking, and once we were on the move the midges didn't bother us.

A rough path runs north from Lone and enters an old, dying pinewood between two huge, split boulders – the portals to the mountain kingdom of Foinaven. But Foinaven wasn't on our agenda for today. Beyond the twin boulder portals the footpath runs up to a high bealach, the Bealach Horn, a marvellous mountain cradle that connects three separate mountains – Arkle to the west, Foinaven to the north-west and Meall Horn to the east. Steep western slopes drop down to a series of mountain tarns that eventually merge with the lochan-speckled moors south-east of Rhiconich, a landscape where it's hard to tell whether it's a loch covered in islands, or a bog full of ponds!

Although it's possible to climb the three Corbetts in one very long day, we were content with climbing Arkle before descending to the Bealach Horn where we would find a campsite, pitch the tent, then climb Meall Horn as a bit of after-dinner exercise.

The one drawback, perhaps, to walking in high summer. The wind only has to drop and the midges come out to feed ... and they take no hostages.

Chaffinch song from the old pine trees worked its healing magic after our ordeal with the midges, and the view of Ben Stack across the waters of its loch had me reaching for my camera. From the winding path a great rising escarpment of Cambrian quartzite stretched to the west, culminating in what appeared to be a flat-topped stony wedge, the eastern summit slopes of Arkle, or Arcuil, at 787 metres.

The zig-zag path climbed the hillside before entering the hidden, steep-sided glen of Allt Horn. The start of a relatively flat section signalled it was time to leave the comfort of the path and take to the heather, or in this case, the broad, stony south-south-east ridge of Arkle. As we climbed the ridge, keeping the burn that crashes downhill from Meall Aonghais on our right, we flirted with the clouds and played peek-a-boo with the views. White-rumped wheatears flitted along in front, leading us upwards, and from somewhere close by the mournful sound of a golden plover reminded us of our hills of home, the high Cairngorms and Monadh Liath.

After a couple of kilometres of relatively easy climbing we sensed, through the mists, that we were approaching a top of sorts. The breeze had picked up and we had become aware, with a hillwalker's sixth sense, that we were approaching the edge of something. Someone once told me that man originally had something like several dozen natural senses but other than the five we use regularly – smell, sight, touch, hearing and taste – the others lie dormant in our brain, unused and unpractised. Occasionally, circumstances rouse these dormant senses into action, senses that we often attribute to outside forces, or some kind of interventionist help from spiritual or supernatural sources.

I remember being on a hill with a deerstalker friend who suddenly bid me to be quiet and crawl forward slowly. "There's deer just over the ridge crest," he told me confidently. He was right. I later asked him how he knew. "Instinct," was all he said.

Doug Scott, the great mountaineer who, along with Dougal Haston, became the first Brits to stand on the summit of Everest, has an instinctive sense of danger, a sense that he has never allowed to wither and atrophy because of lack of use. This instinct, or a simple gut-reaction, can be an important tool in your navigation arsenal too – the 'feeling' that you're heading in the wrong direction should never be completely disregarded. You might just find it's an inherent navigational 'sense' that you just don't use very much.

Autumn storms roll in on Arkle – seen here from south of Loch Stack.

f *White-rumped wheatears flitted along in front, leading us upwards, and from somewhere close by the mournful sound of a golden plover reminded us of our hills of home, the high Cairngorms and Monadh Liath.* ™

As it was, the top we felt we were approaching was real enough and soon the ground broke away from below our feet to reveal dizzying depths into the corrie of Am Bàthaich. Arkle's finest feature is the magnificent half-mile ridge that sweeps gracefully round the lip of this east-facing corrie, connecting its two summits. This high quartzite walkway narrows appreciably in places, with steep drops on either side, before rising to the stony summit and, by the time we reached it, now that the early clouds and vapours had been whisked away by the breeze, a wonderful viewpoint.

Below our feet a number of mountain tarns and lochans created a string of shining levels down towards Rhiconich. Beyond them, Cambrian quartzite slopes rose to the long ridge of what is probably the finest mountain in this empty quarter, the Queen of Sutherland – Foinaven. Some readers might remember the racehorses named after these two mountains – Arkle and Foinavon. (I'm not sure why the Duchess of Westminster, who owned the horses, mis-spelled the latter.) I once met a rather drunken climber in the bar of Glen Coe's Clachaig Inn who tried hard to persuade me that the hills were actually named after the racehorses!

To the east the relatively anonymous top of Meall Horn, the other Corbett in this Sutherland triumvirate, rose above the Bealach Horn, the high point in a long, curvaceous ridge between Creagan Meall Horn and Sàbhal Mor.

In rapidly improving weather we looped back round the summit ridge and retraced our steps back to the Bealach Horn footpath. A small lochan, just a little north-east of Lochan na Faoileige, is set high above two larger lochans, Loch an Easain Uaine and Loch na Tuadh, which are cradled in different levels of the huge, impressive corrie that is shared by both Arkle and Foinaven. We found a flat stretch of turf beside this small lochan and, with much of the afternoon left to play with, took our time in putting on a brew, pitching the tent, and settling in to what was the finest camp of the trip.

Later, after supper, we climbed back to the footpath and made our way up grassy slopes past a band of black, dripping crags, to the broad ridge that connects Creagan Meall Horn with the rounded, wind-clipped 777 metre summit of Meall Horn. A rocky spine led down to the bare, remote upper confines of Glen Golly and to the north lay the narrow lairig of Strath Dionard, a long gash between the east-facing crags of Foinaven and the steeper cliffline of Cranstackie's south ridge. Wild, remote, rugged, bare – it's difficult to find the words to describe this northern arm of those landscapes that have been created by the Moine Thrust, a waterlogged mattress of knolls and lochans that spreads out towards Loch Eriboll and Loch Hope. The whole scene is both ominous and dark, the lower hills lying like brooding witches, their gullies, ribs and ridges all pulsating with an ancient aura, older than words can describe or imaginations conceive.

Eventually Gina had to drag me away from the edge. Black clouds were forming in the west and curtains of rain were already sweeping towards us from the south-west. We made it back to the tent with only minutes to spare before the rain fell.

FOINAVEN – THE QUEEN OF SUTHERLAND

The name of Foinaven has a number of different possible derivations. It been translated as 'the big wedge', and if you look towards it over the waters of Loch Laxford in the west you can begin to understand the thinking behind that name. Leviathan in size, its western aspect is bulky with steeply rounded, vertiginous slopes that can look curiously Himalayan when covered in snow.

An alternative translation suggests the hill was named after Fionn MacCumhail, the fabled Celtic warrior and head of the Fianna warriors. A third translation suggests Fionn, the 'fair' or 'white' hill. However, it's now generally agreed that Foinaven is an anglicisation of *foinne-bheinn*, meaning 'wart mountain', a reference to the many bumps on its ridge.

From the Bealach Horn, Foinaven appears as a narrow north–south rough quartzite ridge stretching for over three kilometres above the 800 metre contour. The highest point, just north of the mid-point, is Ganu Mòr. West of the ridge, steep scree slopes fall to a glacier-scoured, lochan-studded seaboard. To the east, three impressive corries separate ridges that fall into Strath Dionard whose river gathers the tumbling waters of a thousand waterfalls and flows north to the Kyle of Durness and the open sea.

Leaving our tent to be dismantled on our return, we climbed back to the footpath and followed it up to the 500 metre contour. Beyond that point the path curves round to the north of Creagan Meall Horn and drops down into the upper reaches of Glen Golly and then down to Gobernuisgach Lodge where it meets up with our planned route from Lone – through Srath Luib na Seillich and over the Bealach na Fèithe. This higher-level route makes a good alternative for Sutherland Trail walkers who want to climb Foinaven en route.

We left the path at its high point and made for the crest of the long ridge that forms the eastern skyline of Coir' a' Chruiteir and culminates in the An t-Sàil Mhor top, often referred to as Craig Dionard, at 778 metres. We skirted west of the summit on slopes of stone and scree and were delighted to find purple moss campion growing in small bright clumps amid the stony desolation of this high tundra-like landscape. To our left, at the head of Coir' a' Chruiteir, a broad grassy platform curved round to gently climb to Foinaven's 808 metre top, Stob Cadha na Beucaich, high above the Cadha na Beucaich ('the pass of the bellowing'), and the start of the mountain's main ridge.

From this high point the character of the mountain changes. All the way from our camp we had wandered in a desultory fashion up broad ridges, searching for wild flowers and delighting in the views of Arkle's big corries to the south. We had lain down on swards of grass and gazed south and west, way beyond the hills that we had climbed or passed in the days since leaving Lochinver. It had been a relaxed hour or so but now, at the head of a steep and loose rocky shute that led down to the Cadha na Beucaich, I could sense the difference in the atmosphere.

Carrying less than five kilograms, Cameron has everything he needs (including a small bottle of wine) for this overnight camp.

The main ridge of Foinaven is composed of shattered quartzite and offers a long, high, steep and grey face to the main road on the west coast. The steep corries and side spurs that give the mountain its unique character are hidden on the eastern side. The quartzite screes are loose and steep and, apparently shift continually, giving a constant background sound of tumbling rocks on a still day. I think it was the mountain photographer-cum-Yardley's perfumier, Walter Poucher, who came up with this rather fanciful notion that you could sit up here and enjoy a somewhat eerie experience by listening to disintegrating quartzite blocks falling from the crags. Sure, there is erosion, but the mountain isn't peeling away that badly!

But it was the erosion of the summit path that was worrying Gina. I could sense her trepidation as we began a slow and very careful descent. Three years ago she slipped on some ice at about 5,200 metres on the Thorung La in the Annapurna range in Nepal and broke an ankle. A year later she slipped on some greasy wet grass outside a holiday house in Morven and broke the other one. She's been ultra-careful, and not a little fearful, ever since. I guess I can't blame her.

If you take care the descent doesn't pose any real difficulties, provided you don't knock stones down on the person below you! Despite Gina's initial trepidation we were down on the pass in no time at all, taking a break by the tiny stone shelter that decorates the saddle of the Cadha na Beucaich. Another steep climb lay in front of us – up to a prominent peak known as Lord Reay's Seat, a black, craggy prominence not unlike Lord Berkeley's Seat on An Teallach.

The summit of the Seat can easily be bypassed on the left before a short traverse to the A' Ch'eir Ghorm top, which sends out a long and narrow roof-like spur to the east, one of the most remarkable features of Foinaven. From here I could sense Gina relaxing again, the difficulties behind us, and an easy, if undulating, ridge before us. A slight descent, another climb over an un-named top and a long and tight curving ridge took us to the broad summit slopes and an easy climb to the plateau-like high point, Ganu Mòr ('the big head'), with its twin cairns.

Between clouds that seemed determined to wrap themselves around Foinaven's airy tops, we glimpsed Cape Wrath, the most north-westerly corner of the UK, just a few

Looking west on a landscape that seems composed as much of water as solid land.

miles away beyond the sprawling, low-lying area known as the Parph. Close by rose the Corbetts of Cranstackie and Beinn Spionnaidh, the most northerly in the land, two hills that I climbed about a dozen years ago with Rebecca Ridgway on one of my *Wilderness Walks* television programmes. Ben Hope and Ben Loyal looked a long distance away in the blue east, with Morven in Caithness even more distant. Closer at hand, to the south and west beyond Arkle, lay Ben Stack, Quinag, Ben More Assynt and Conival, Canisp and Suilven – the hills of the Sutherland Trail.

Enraptured by it all, we sat by the westerly cairn and ate our lunch, looking out to sea beyond the indented islands of Loch Laxford and past the seabird reserve of Handa. We peered through the shifting mists at a scene that is so unique to this place called Sutherland, the South Land of the Viking jarls, the genuine land of the mountain and the flood, the 'empty lands' of the Victorians and the modern romantics.

It was good to sit here, in the easy and comfortable silence between two like-minded folk, two-as-one alone on a remote mountain top and well removed from whatever may have been happening in the wider world. We just didn't want to know. Our world lay immediately around us, in all its starkness and its magnificence and we were content simply to wonder at the natural beauty and mystery of it all.

I guess 'wonder' is a slightly old-fashioned word. People tend not to talk about 'wonder' any more, as if we know everything there is to know. Indeed hillwalkers and climbers often write as though they have a privileged insight as to what makes up this amorphous thing we call landscape and go on to write in a language that only the enlightened will understand. The poet William Blake once called on us to learn how to see for ourselves. "For to see," he said, "was the beginning of wonder." And so often the outcome of this wonder is a sense of gratitude, an appreciation of whatever or whoever put together this complete intricate jigsaw that the great John Muir once described as "the eternal web of creation", a web that we are also part of and to which we also belong.

We eventually dragged ourselves away and retreated back along the ridge, to return along the shifting screes and rocks to the summit of Stob Cadha na Beucaich. We both felt curiously lighter and more at ease with our surroundings than we did earlier. Perhaps, after the wonder of revelation at the summit, we felt more of a kinship with the hill and the lochans and the streams and the clumps of moss campion, more aware that we are simply part and parcel of such landscapes, part of the rock and the light and the air and the waters of pre-life. Content enough in that knowledge, we ambled back down towards the tent, packed everything away, and followed the path back to Lone and another riverside camp.

Munro status or not, Foinaven will always be a popular hill, but will remain relatively free of the crowds because of its distance from the main centres of population. Three thousand feet or not, it will always be a rather special mountain, a royal mountain – the Queen of Sutherland!

The beauty of the Sutherland Trail isn't confined to vast panoramic views —
it can be seen in close-up details along the way.

LONE TO TONGUE

The ruins of Moine House, west of Tongue, with Ben Loyal in the background. The house has a long history and was once an inn frequented by cattle drovers. A faded wall plaque commemorates the construction of the original road in 1830.

Local folk refer to it as the Burma Road, a hill track that once connected remote communities, providing a route for those seeking work in the fishing industry of the east coast.

After the Second World War, the path between Lone and Gobernuisgach Lodge was widened and improved, and the labourers who carried out the tortuous, midge-bitten work named it after its infamous Far Eastern namesake, the route that links Myanmar with China. Curiously enough, not far from my own home in Badenoch, there's another Burma Road. This one runs over the Monadh Liath between Llynwilg and the Dulnain and its name has similar origins. There's also a Burma Road on Raasay.

The track begins at Lone on the east shore of Loch Stack and winds eastwards through the Srath Luib na Seilich for a distance of some fifteen kilometres, past the Reay Estate's Gobernuisgach Lodge and into the historic Strath More below Ben Hope, the most northerly of Scotland's Munros.

TRAIL INFORMATION

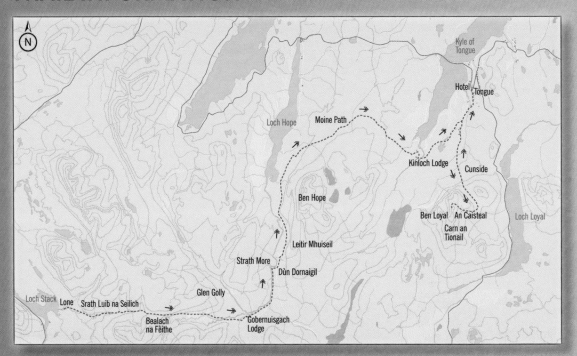

Lone to Tongue

Map
Ordnance Survey 1:50,000 Sheet 9 (Cape Wrath); Sheet 10 (Strath Naver)

Distance
44 kilometres / 26 miles (59 kilometres / 35 miles with ascent of Ben Loyal from road end at Ribigill Farm)

Approx. time
2 days

Terrain
Good paths and tracks; some 0road walking in Strath More on a very quiet, little-used road and between Kinloch and Tongue. Muddy paths and easy river crossing on ascent of Ben Loyal.

Route

From Lone take the track beside the Abhainn an Lòin before climbing up through a narrow gap into Srath Luib Seillich. Continue E as the track rises to the Bealach na Fèithe. Continue E, descending through a patch of forest. Break clear of the forest on a good track and cross the bridge over the Abhainn Srath Coir' an Easaidh. Continue E to a junction, turn left and descend to Gobernuisgach Lodge. Go through the grounds and continue on a good track through a forest, above the river. When you leave the forest the track swings to the right but at the bend leave the track and follow fishermen's paths N beside the Strathmore River. Where the river forms an obvious dogleg climb the slopes to the road at Dùn Dornaigil. Follow the road N for 6 kilometres to the S end of Loch Hope. A footpath, the Moine Path, leaves the road on the right. Follow this path for 13 kilometres to the road at Kinloch. From Kinloch follow the road to Tongue.

To climb Ben Loyal leave the car park at the road end to Ribigill Farm (GR584542) and follow the farm road S through the farm and onto the moors beyond. Continue S over a boggy track past the empty buildings at Cunside. Climb grassy slopes to the Bealach Clais nan Ceap, a wide flat pass that separates the main mountain from the outlier of Ben Heil, then climb steeper grassy slopes to your right to gain the broad summit ridge between Sgòr Chaonasaid and An Caisteal. Continue S on this ridge before bearing right up a granite block. The summit cairn tops this block with sheer drops to the E. Return the same way.

Accommodation

No accommodation between Lone and Tongue but plenty of good wild camping spots.

Tongue Hotel: 01847 611206; www.tonguehotel.co.uk. Slightly more expensive than either Inchnadamph or Kylesku but offering fabulous food and wine. Excellent local staff, a welcoming hotel for the end of a long walk.

Ben Loyal Hotel: 01847 611216; www.benloyal.co.uk. Cosy and friendly hotel with great views of Ben Loyal.

Tongue Youth Hostel: 01847 611 789; www.syha.org.uk/hostels/highlands/tongue. A popular and magnificently situated hostel, just outside the village on the Durness road.

Public transport

There are regular trains between Inverness and Lairg and a Post Bus service between Tongue and Lairg. A Post Bus runs between Tongue and Lairg every day except Sunday, leaving at 08:15 Mon–Fri and 07:45 on a Saturday. The journey takes an hour.

We were out of our sleeping bags, breakfasted and packed up by nine o'clock, aware that we had a fairly long day ahead of us. We hoped to cross the high ground to Strath More and then, all going well, tackle the ten kilometre road walk up the length of Strath More to the start of the Moine Path that would set us off on our final leg to Ben Loyal and Tongue. I'm no lover of walking on tarmac, but we didn't expect to meet much in the way of traffic on this particular road, decorated with grass growing in the middle of it. On a previous occasion, I walked the entire length hoping for a lift. Not one car passed me.

The Bealach na Fèithe track initially follows the lively Abhainn an Lòin before gradually pulling away from the river as it climbs the hillside towards an obvious gap in some low crags. After this initial pull uphill, just enough to get us sweating, the path levels out before dropping into the long Srath Luib na Seilich with the obvious U-shape of the Bealach na Fèithe forming the low point of the hilly horizon ahead of us. On either side of the pass, steep slopes lead to rugged tops – on the left, Sàbhal Beag and the start of a fine, undulating, high-level ridge walk that leads to the Corbett of Meall Horn, and on the right, Meall Garbh and a fabulous high-level stroll above the crags of Coire Loch to the Corbett of Meallan Liath Coire Mhic Dhughaill, which we first glimpsed way back on the path between Kylestrome and Achfary. There is so much good hillwalking in this area that it almost felt like sacrilege to be blasting though the glens on the low-level trails. For the umpteenth time I promised myself a return trip to this area to climb some of these hills that are neither Corbetts nor Munros – the Grahams of Sutherland await.

Before dropping into Srath Luib na Seilich we stopped for a few moments to catch our breath and gaze behind us. Ben Stack towered over the waters of its eponymous loch, steep-sided with a prominent band of vertical crags protecting it from the north, its pyramidal shape slightly blunted by a flat summit. A magnificent hill, yet at 719 metres it doesn't even meet Corbett height, convincing me yet again that these hills of the north-west Highlands should never be judged on height alone.

We had reconnoitred this route earlier in the year on a day of scudding clouds and rain that balanced delicately on the cusp of spring. We had walked from the road by Loch Stack all the way up to the bealach but had hardly seen a thing because of low cloud,

The Abhainn an Lòin near Lone Cottage. The track taken by the route can be seen in the centre background leading up the Srath Luib na Seilich.

but what we did discover was an excellent track that ran all the way up the length of the strath – God bless the workers of Sutherland's Burma Road! Today we were blessed with much better weather. Slightly cooler than it had been of late, the sun shone from between ragged clouds but we did sense a change in the approaching weather. The barometer of my altimeter watch had dropped significantly during the night and we were aware of the high cirrus that was forming in the west. After four days of superb summer weather, a weather pattern that isn't uncommon in the north-west Highlands in early summer, we were not surprised at the prospect of a few showers.

The year before, Gina and I had hiked from Fort William to Cape Wrath, following various tracks and trails that make up the route of the 'unofficial' Cape Wrath Trail. While the rest of the UK suffered rainstorms of almost biblical proportions, we wandered along, day after day, for over two weeks, with hardly a drop of rain, cursing the fact that we had carried waterproofs all the way and never had to use them. You just can't please some folk …

However, the weather suddenly changed as we approached the Cape Wrath lighthouse and it was an eerie experience to take photographs of each other beside the lighthouse as we peered through thick fog. A curious bank of cloud enveloped the immediate area of the lighthouse, and when we boarded the minibus to take us to the ferry to cross the Kyle of Durness we drove out of the cloud in just a few minutes. Despite that odd meteorological experience it certainly isn't unusual for the north-west to enjoy good weather in the spring and early summer. When I returned to Sutherland later in the year for another couple of weeks to film the route for the television show, we enjoyed very settled weather for all but a couple of days of drizzle.

Disused gates and abandoned fencing are silent witnesses to the work that once went on in this landscape.

From Lone, it is about six kilometres to the top of the pass, six kilometres along a broad and not unpleasant glen with steep corrie-bitten hills on either side. A herd of hinds, about a hundred of them, moved slowly across a distant hillside like the shadow of a slow-moving cloud. Wheatears bobbed on boulders ahead of us before flying off to the next boulder where the bobbing routine would begin ahead – it was as though they were personally leading us up the glen towards the Bealach na Fèithe, a flat, peat-hagged place with bog-cotton blowing in the breeze and the crumbling remains of some ancient building reminding us that all kinds of folk – tramps, vagabonds, clansmen, soldiers, priests and poets – have traversed this route since time immemorial.

CROSSING THE WATERSHED

Although it may have been scenically underwhelming compared to some of the landscapes we had passed through, this high pass represented a watershed on the Sutherland Trail, the crossing of a divide, from the north-west coast where the culture and ancient language is that of the Western Isles into a land where the traditional influences have their origins in Norse. We were also approaching a district where the hills of the west would dwindle out towards the Flow Country of Caithness, a land that is as physically different from the western seaboard as you could imagine, but nevertheless a land with its own attractions and attributes. East of a line between Ben Hee and Ben Loyal lies an area of Flow Country, much altered by insensitive commercial forestry, but still exciting to visit. Greenshanks arrive here from North Africa to breed in the spring, using the same nesting sites each year. Golden plover and dunlin join them. Buzzards, hen harriers and peregrines rule the moorlands. The rarely seen wildcats roam here too, and the trout-filled lochs provide natural larders for otters and attract fly-fishermen from all over the world.

To put the cultural difference in its most basic form, the people of north-west Sutherland will drive to Ullapool for their shopping, whereas the people on the east side of this bealach will go to Thurso. As I stopped just short of the summit of the pass I realised

❝ *Buzzards, hen harriers and peregrines rule the moorlands.* ❞

that this divide was also part of the watershed of Scotland, the ancient Druim Alban, the spine of the land, the physical barrier that once separated the ancient Scots from the Picts. Behind us the streams and burns and rivers all flowed to the western seas. Ahead of us the general direction of the watercourses would be east, and then north to the Pentland Firth. The big hills of Meall Horn, Foinaven, Cranstackie and Beinn Spionnaidh form the north–south spine, part of the Moine Thrust, that divides one region from the other.

There are almost limitless opportunities for adding additional summits to those along the Sutherland Trail. The road north to Durness provides excellent views of both Beinn Spionnaidh (773 metres) and its taller neighbour Cranstackie (801 metres) – a memorable outing.

The geographical symbolism of this pass wasn't lost on us, even though the cultural differences between the lands on either side of it may not be as great as they once were, but my guess is that the vast majority of mountaineers, climbers, hillwalkers and backpackers who go to the mountains and wild places of Scotland very rarely consider the word 'culture' as part of their game. There may well be a subliminal understanding of a cultural aspect to their activity, or they may be aware that the likes of Wordsworth and Coleridge, or Henry David Thoreau and John Muir were stimulated in their literature by the landscapes they experienced, but for most hillgoers, it seems, the most immediate concern is in the physical challenge, the titillation of the senses and a sense of achievement. Or, as I've read on one hillwalker's blog, the whole experience is no more than a good day out with the lads.

I have to admit that my own awareness of culture in the mountains was pretty limited until about a dozen years ago. By 'limited awareness' I mean that, while I was aware of the cultural connections between our landscapes and art, music, literature and photography, I just hadn't considered those connections very deeply, and I guess that's the same for most folk. However, a dozen years ago I took a walk in Skye, from Sligachan to Elgol by way of Loch Coruisk, with Donnie Munro, the one-time lead singer of the folk-rock band Runrig.

During that walk with Donnie, filmed as part of my *Wilderness Walks* series, I realised just how much of his life had been shaped by the landscape of Skye and in particular, the Cuillin. For a time, Donnie had been a member of the Skye Mountain Rescue Team. He was also an artist, having trained at Gray's School of Art in Aberdeen and had been an art teacher. Donnie had a profound love of the Gaelic language and culture, and of course, a love of singing and music. Indeed, Donnie told me that the vast majority of the music written by the MacDonald brothers in Runrig had been inspired by the landscapes of the Western Isles.

Encouraged by Donnie, I looked more deeply into the idea of a connection between the mountain and culture, and realised that the great Gaelic bard Somhairle MacGill-Eain (Sorley MacLean) had been equally inspired by the landscape of the Cuillin. In a poem describing the homecoming of Gaels after the war, he refers to the Cuillin peaks as

Autumn colours and changing weather highlight this ruin at the head of Strath More.

"the mother breasts of the world, erect with the universe's concupiscence." Here lies the very heart of Gaeldom, he wrote, "the white felicity of the high towered mountains", beckoning the Gaels to their homeland.

It's interesting that when the late John MacLeod of MacLeod put the Skye Cuillin on the open market for a cool £10 million in the mid-1990s, many local Skye people made their own claim on the Cuillin, referring to it as a 'cultural' claim, as distinct from the 'emotional' claim to ownership that many mountaineers felt. I guess it all boils down to a perceived sense of belonging.

If someone were to ask me where I most belonged I'd have little hesitation in saying the Cairngorms. These are the landscapes with which I have greatest familiarity, and I've spent 30 years living in their shadow. The time I've spent immersed in the place has given me an experiential knowledge of the hills and corries and plateaux that has been vitally important in forming and developing this sense of belonging. I'm convinced that the wild lands that surround us help shape our culture, and the more we despoil, or even lose, aspects of that wild land then we increasingly run the risk of shifting our society into a 'placelessness' where culture and history become unimportant and we, as a society, begin to lose our sense of identity. I'm also well aware that many of these landscapes have not always been devoid of man, that the whispers and taints of man's existence are still there, to feel and to see and to experience. And that brings me to the concept of 'spirit of place'.

There have been times when walking on this trail, and in particular I think of leaning against the old gable wall of the shieling remains above Achfary, when I've distinctly experienced the impressions that have been left behind by generations of people. I've become aware that people have lived there before me, have loved there, have laughed there, have died there, have had children who played there. And it's nothing to do with the 'wilderness' that we like to think it is nowadays. These landscapes may be comparatively empty now but it's vital for me, as a Scot, to remind myself that people used to live here before the lands were emptied. And to me that is all part of the fabric of the Scottish mountains, and part of the culture of Scotland. The consequences of ignoring the importance of 'place' are only too easy to imagine, as are the implications of placelessness.

And if we alter these landscapes so much that we lose this sense of 'spirit of place' we are in danger of losing something vital. In 1987, W. H. Murray, speaking of the Cairngorm plateau, suggested those landscapes had the ability to "cast a spell on the mind" but he also remarked: "Every man-made road driven to the interior, and every building put there, diminishes that experience. The process has gone too far and should be halted; the loss is becoming irreparable."

Wise words from one of our most prophetic mountain writers, but very few folk today value such wild places in aesthetic, or philosophical, terms. Even fewer value them in cultural terms. Encouragingly, the annual Fort William Mountain Festival have instituted an annual award for those who have contributed substantially to "the mountain culture of Scotland" and I'm delighted that my old friend and co-author of this book, Richard Else, was the most recent recipient of this award for his long list of television programmes that reflect the diversity and enduring appeal of the Scottish Highlands as a destination for adventure sports and activities.

Abandoned croft houses are a feature of the Sutherland landscape.

❝ … if we alter these landscapes so much that we
lose this sense of 'spirit of place' we are in danger of
losing something vital. ❞

STRATHMORE AND DÙN DORNAIGIL

Curiously, both Gina and I sensed a difference in the atmosphere of the landscape as we descended from the Bealach na Fèithe above the Abhainn Srath Coir' an Easaidh. It might have been the change in the weather or perhaps the fragrant tang of salt air had gone – I'm not too sure what it was but we seemed to be descending into what appeared to be a parched land where the old trees, with little or no new growth, looked worn and tired. The deer fencing around the woodland had collapsed in places, the old footpath was waterworn and looked to be in need of repair here and there. Grey clouds had drifted into the high corries and blanketed the summits and the slopes appeared grim and forbidding as they rose gauntly into the mists.

For some reason we both felt a little depressed, deflated, and we couldn't quite shake it off. Perhaps it was something to do with the weather; perhaps we were subconsciously aware that we had a stretch of tarmac-bashing later in the afternoon; maybe the bitter-sweet reaction to completing a long walk was hitting us a day early; or could there be something in the spirit of the land itself, or some evil event from the past that still resonates down the decades? I once had a dog, a beautifully tempered black Labrador, who habitually cowered and whimpered whenever we passed a particular stretch of road in our local glen. I've absolutely no idea why …

A footbridge carried us over the lively waters of the Abhainn Srath Coir' an Easaidh and we sat on some wooden logs by the forest and put on a brew. The gloominess still hung heavy on us and Gina tried to brighten things up by telling me of the meal she was planning the next night in the Tongue Hotel – French onion soup, warm freshly baked bread, scallops, fillet of venison and chocolate éclairs with fresh cream. All washed down with a good bottle of Shiraz. I brought her back to earth with the menu for tonight's dinner – pasta and cheese!

In contrast to the tired feel of the glen behind us, Gobernuisgach Lodge and its grounds look well kept and manicured. Three cars were parked in front of the big house and we stopped for a moment and chatted to the keeper. He remarked on how good the weather had been but reminded us that a change was in store. "I think you'll be fine tonight," he said, "but tomorrow might be a bit damp."

A long stretch of track through more woodland brought us to the Strathmore River and its little fishermen's huts. This river, which drains over 200 square kilometres of mountainous country, is formed by three small streams rising in the old Reay Forest, not very far from Gobernuisgach Lodge. The Strathmore River flows through Strath More under the birch-clad slopes of Ben Hope for some twelve kilometres, when it expands into Loch Hope – a lovely sheet of water nearly ten kilometres long, and varying from two hundred to twelve hundred metres in width.

According to the map, we had to follow a big bend in the track to climb up to the main road which we'd then use to tramp through Strath More, but on an instinct we decided to leave the main track and follow a little footpath beside the river. If fishermen used this river a lot there would be a path-of-sorts alongside it, and there was, for over two kilometres, to a distinct and sudden dogleg in the river, just below the imposing ruins of the Dùn Dornaigil broch, one of the best surviving examples of a circular defensive tower of the Iron Age.

Scotland's most northerly Munro, Ben Hope, and the tiny community around Alltnacaillich, seen from the Strathmore River.

THE MYSTERY OF BROCHS

Although it is but a remnant of its former splendour we weren't disappointed. The drystone wall is almost perfectly circular, three metres thick at the base and rising to a height of nearly ten metres. Its walls would have been hollow with a stone staircase inside giving access to galleries, which were probably used for storage. The inner courtyard has a diameter of some seven to ten metres and would have been covered with a thatched roof, although today the inside is filled with rubble and weeds. Only a small, low doorway, with a curious triangular shaped lintel, suggested an entry point. Who were the people who built this dun, this fort, and why? Was it to offer protection from an enemy? There are about five hundred brochs left in Scotland, and the broch builders were most likely to have been the Picts, but were the brochs built as defensive forts, or as some form of farming settlement?

Dùn Dornaigil broch dates from the Iron Age and although it is not possible to enter it, it is still a spectacular sight in the lonely but beautiful Strath More glen.

Archaeology casts little light on the matter. If the brochs were defensive structures, who was the enemy? The Iron Age in Scotland is reckoned to have been around 450 BC to 400 AD, which would seem to rule out the Norsemen as enemies. There wasn't even an organised civilisation in Norway in such far-off days. Having said that, rock carvings that depict longships, dated 1000 BC and earlier, have been found in Norway and Sweden. Is it possible that bands of unorganised Vikings sailed the northern seas in expeditions of plunder long before the establishment of a kingdom in Scandinavia? The early Vikings kept no written records, but if the broch people had an enemy, then history points the finger at the Vikings.

However, modern historians would tell you that no weapons have been found in the vicinity of the brochs, and there is no archival indication that the broch dwellers used the structures purely for defensive reasons. And you'd think that if the brochs had been built as some kind of defensive fortification they would have been built on the top of a hill. Few of them were, and indeed, the Dùn Dornaigil lies in the middle of a broad strath, close to the river. Some archaeologists believe that they were simply 'status symbols', a visible demonstration that a particular settlement or group of farmers were wealthy and successful. The broch was originally known as Dùn Dornadilla, but in the late 19th century was referred to as Dùn Dornaigil. Dornadille was an early Scottish king. Could there be a connection? Who knows …?

BEN HOPE

Content to let the mystery be, we enjoyed a twenty minute break by the ruins, imagining life all these years ago. Whoever lived here had chosen a marvellous spot. The fast-flowing river leads the eye from the ruins along the broad strath to where steep cliffs tumble down from Ben Hope. Indeed, there isn't much of Scotland left beyond Ben Hope. While neighbouring Ben Loyal stands a little further north, Ben Hope is our most northerly Munro at a height of 927 metres and can be climbed from Strath More up the burn just north of the Dùn Dornaigil, which leads to the upper southern slopes.

From the north Ben Hope appears as a crag-girt wedge, but most folk climb the hill from the west by the signposted path that leaves the road three kilometres north of Dùn

Ben Hope viewed from the start of the road by Loch Hope. Even today this small road is still so little used that grass grows in its centre and walkers can wander down it undisturbed.

Dornaigil, and takes a meandering route past a series of cascading waterfalls to steeper, craggier slopes where a sly line breaks through a weakness in the western escarpment to deliver you on the bare, stony summit slopes. A well-worn footpath scours its way uphill, twisting and turning past the inevitable piles of waymarking cairns.

But even the petty works of homo constructus can't compete with the sense of isolation that eases off into its watery wilderness far below. The long thin arm of Loch Hope leads the eye north to the open sea and to the east the multi-topped outline of Ben Loyal sings defiantly of the wonder and fascination of mountains, no matter how far above or below any of man's imposed plimsoll lines.

The more adventurous scrambler may wish to climb Ben Hope from the north. This route involves a walk-in from the head of Loch Hope towards the Dubh-loch na Beinne, a lochan which is situated just below the mountain's north-western crags. Above the dark waters you can climb fairly easily to the mountain's north ridge where a ten metre section offers some exhilarating scrambling to the summit. The most difficult section can be avoided on the left (east) by climbing a gully that leads to the ridge higher up.

ON THE MOUNTAIN WITH GRIFF RHYS JONES

As we hobbled along the tarmac road, midge-bitten and sweltering in the afternoon heat, past the sign that pointed to Ben Hope, I couldn't help but contrast the weather conditions with the last time I climbed the hill. Blizzards and low temperatures had caused chaos on Highland and Grampian roads. The far north of Scotland was experiencing the kind of winter weather that now seems like a distant memory.

A few miles to the south-east, the Altnaharra Inn recorded the lowest temperatures in the country – minus sixteen degrees Celsius – and the moors of Sutherland resembled all the empty grimness of a Siberian landscape. Occasionally, through the driving snows you could just discern the turret-like shapes of Ben Loyal's peaks and across the Kyle of Tongue, the great wedge-shaped nose of Ben Hope broke free only when the weather fronts graced us with a brief interlude between the racing clouds.

For this wintry ascent I was the guest of the BBC and television personality Griff Rhys Jones who hoped to climb his very first hill for a television series called *Mountain*. His introductory hill was well named …

Because of nightmarish logistics and the difficulties of transporting a film crew along snow-blasted Highland roads, we didn't start climbing Ben Hope until lunchtime, hoping that the weather fronts would space themselves out sufficiently to give us the occasional glimpse of winter mountain scenery. We left the roadside in Strath More with me anxiously checking my watch, seriously concerned about a lack of daylight hours, and Griff twittering on about spaceships and mountain spirits. According to some curious religious sect he had read about, Ben Hope is apparently a holy mountain.

For someone who had never climbed higher than the restaurant in London's Post Office Tower, Griff did extremely well and blasted his way up knee-deep snow slopes with great gusto. The old credo about walking at a pace that allowed you to have a conversation seemed to have an adverse effect on Griff. I reckoned he could still garble away nineteen to the dozen even if he was running uphill flat-out!

Because we had to stop every so often and be filmed, our progress was slow, but between the snow showers the sun broke through to turn the white, windswept desolation into a scene of Alpine purity, sparklingly bright and pristine. Like an advert for spring water, Griff suggested.

I silently prayed that our arrival at the summit trig point would coincide with one of these clear spells but it wasn't to be. By the time we climbed over onto the edge of the summit plateau we were in a whiteout. Visibility was reduced to a few feet and we had to navigate the short distance to the summit and its ice-rimed trig point.

Thankfully my navigation was spot-on.

Delighting in his first Munro summit I told Griff that the first man to climb all the Munros, the Reverend A. E. Robertson, climbed his final Munro and kissed the cairn, then his wife, in celebration. Perhaps Griff would like to kiss the cairn of his first Munro? He declined, imagining the potential newspaper headlines that reported a well-known television celebrity stuck to a frozen mountain cairn by his tongue. I had only suggested he kiss the cairn, but I guess he made a fair point.

We descended in the dark by the light of our head torches and Griff was unusually quiet. It had been something of a baptism of ice for him, the first of a number of hills that he would climb in the course of the five-part series, the beginning of a year-long odyssey over the mountains of Britain. On the way back to Tongue in the car he looked stiff and uncomfortable and complained of a sore back. I couldn't help but wonder if he'd survive the series …

The Moine Path to Kinloch

By the time Gina and I reached the start of the Moine Path, at the south end of Loch Hope, I was in the bad books. The long haul on the unforgiving tarmac had taken it out of her and to make matters worse, the only car that we had met on the road had actually stopped and offered us a lift. Gina was about to accept when I said no, rather too forcibly I suspect. She stomped off in high dudgeon.

I had promised to camp as soon as we found a reasonable place – a bit of flat grassy ground with water nearby, but there wasn't anywhere suitable, at least not until we reached the southern shores of Loch Hope. Here a footpath sloped off to the right through some gorse bushes, and just beyond a stream that dropped down Ben Hope's cliffs lay a large and welcoming patch of green sward. Rather than show some pleasure at stopping for the night Gina suggested I'd had no intention of stopping earlier. Ho-hum … After 35 years of marriage I knew the best thing to do was keep quiet and not argue.

To add insult to injury, I had just pitched the tent when the rain come on, sweeping up the length of the glen on a warm wind, threatening to soak everything in sight. We threw our packs inside and Gina clambered in after them, but not before giving me

Ben Hope is often regarded as one of the less interesting Munros but this in-spate waterfall on its western flanks shows that there is still much to delight the eye.

the water bottles to fill up. I didn't mind. It was good to be here. It had been a long day and I was ready for a meal and hot drink and then a long sleep before our final day on the Sutherland Trail.

Consider if you will those far-off days when our hills and mountains were regarded as wild areas of desolation and abomination rather than the arenas of recreation they are viewed as today. Closely associated with such landscapes were Celts and Fingalians, Iron Age traders and Roman soldiers, Redcoats and Jacobites, road builders and clansmen, poets and artists. Robbers, poachers, illicit distillers and even political adversaries would take refuge in the remoteness, hiding from the authorities of the day, and spiritual men often found sanctuary here, withdrawing from society to create a peaceful haven in which they could find fellowship with their God.

It's intriguing to stand on a mountain top and look around at the apparently empty lands that lie below. It's a fanciful thought, but one I'm sure that most hillgoers are familiar with, that we often feel we could be the first person ever to stand there. It's even more overwhelming to realise that man has been climbing these hills and criss-crossing those areas we would consider as wilderness since time immemorial – which makes a mockery of any suggestion that such land is private and we have no right to be there. Tell that to the ghosts of yesterday, to the holy men, to the Pictish warriors, to the cattle drovers and the navvy soldiers, the artists and the poets and the writers, the precursors of the hillwalkers and the climbers and the skiers and the ornithologists. The tradition of access is inviolate, inextricably tied up in the comings and goings of centuries of human movement and settlement.

These thoughts went through my mind as we packed up on a drizzly, dour morning and set out on the Moine Path to Kinloch on the Kyle of Tongue. The rough trail was sketchy in places and I hoped against hope that it wouldn't vanish altogether for we were crossing a bare and rather bleak stretch of moorland which, I'm sure, would have been alive with wildlife and on a good day with grand views south to the bulwark end of Ben Hope. But low mist and cloud obscured any distant detail – we were walking in a shroud of sodden grey, a wet vacuum of mist, and in its silent swirl it was all too easy to imagine the people of the land climbing up here with their carts, grunting with the

In countryside this remote, it's often hard to imagine previous generations working here but drystone dykes such as this were painstakingly crafted, often over inhospitable land.

effort of digging the black, oily peat from the ground, loading it and carrying it back to their turf-rooved black-houses. I wonder if the increasing cost of fuel will encourage the Highlander of today back onto the peat roads and peat banks of their forefathers?

But who actually built this path? Here and there it was obviously 'floated' across the bogs, bridges crossed some of the streams and much hard work and effort had gone into its creation. Translated, the Moine Path could mean the 'moss' path. It might even be the 'peat' road – the cart track used by crofters to carry the cut peat from the higher moors. But the most likely origin of the name is its geological position along the Moine Thrust. According to my friend, local angler and writer Bruce Sandison, the path is relatively unused these days.

Bruce told me that on a good day it was a glorious path, with an astonishing array of flora and fauna to be enjoyed along the way. He and his wide Ann often tramp along it on botanical expeditions and to reach some of the remote trout lochs on the east side of Ben Hope. "We arrange to be dropped off at the Loch Hope end and then walk back home, a distance of about eleven miles in about six or seven hours depending upon how often you stop along the way," Bruce told me.

Unfortunately there is little record about when and why the Moine Path was built. However, given that until the early 1800s there were virtually no roads at all in Sutherland, tracks such as the Moine Path, and the path we had followed earlier from Lone to Gobernuisgach, must have been major travel routes used by the majority of the local community to move about the county. In the aftermath of the Sutherland Clearances, the Sutherland Estate made great efforts to open up the county, largely inspired by the public outrage they faced because of the harshness of the Clearances (which earned the Sutherland family an infamous reputation). According to Bruce this was possibly one of the country's first organised public relations attempts at spin and damage limitation!

An expertly built bridge carries the path across high ground.

The expansion of trade and industry in Sutherland resulting from the Clearances coincided with the rise and rise of the herring fishing industry at Wick. By the end of the 19th century, Wick had become the most important fishing station in Europe. To succeed, the herring industry depended upon two primary factors: the presence each summer of the herring, of course, and the availability of something like 5,000 Highland men and women to crew the boats and clean and process the catch.

These men and women came predominantly from the west, from Durness down to Lochinver, and they walked all the way from their home villages and hamlets to Wick. Given the position of the Moine Path, it's a fair assumption that it must have been used by people coming mainly from Scourie and Kinlochbervie, along the Sutherland Estate (now the Westminster Estate) tracks to Loch Hope, and, probably, from the end of the Moine Path to Tongue and along the north coast.

Those from Durness may have taken the more direct route, for them, along the top of Sutherland to the Kyle of Tongue, which would probably be crossed by ferry, and then on into Caithness. From Lochinver, the easiest route would be out to Ledmore and up and down into Strath Oykel, then to Rosehall and Lairg and so on, before heading north up the east coast.

In the early 20th century, when the Westminster Estates acquired their chunk of west Sutherland, they began to develop the old tracks as stalking paths – including, eventually, the Burma Road. Before that, it is almost certain that the tracks were used as drove roads, when cattle were taken to markets in Wick and Lairg. It's likely that the Moine Path would have been one of the most important parts of the route from west to east, avoiding the barrier of the Kyle of Tongue, although in those days, the drovers used to make their cattle swim across stretches of water.

66 *... it is still more horrid when it carries natives who have taken too much whisky, and who produce bottles of it from their pockets and suck at them until they are incapable!* **99**

Even today, there are more hill tracks than public roads in this part of the Highlands. For many years, the main mode of transport was the Post Bus service, but this has been seriously reduced in recent years. A local angler, Duncan Ross, wrote of his experiences in 1889:

> *On the day I wished to quit Tongue, the dogcarts had all gone to the various hill lochs with the trout-fishers, so I had perforce to make my first acquaintance with Her Majesty's mailcart, and in it I started from Tongue to Erribol Ferry, en route to Durness, a cheap and comfortable ride of some twenty-six miles for six shillings, with a tip of half a crown to the well-mannered driver. The same journey in a dogcart would have cost thirty-nine shillings, so from this time forward I often tried the same method of progression, sometimes successfully, sometimes disastrously. A crowded mailcart on a wet day is horrid, and whatever the weather, it is still more horrid when it carries natives who have taken too much whisky, and who produce bottles of it from their pockets and suck at them until they are incapable!*

The rain persisted as we tramped across the moorlands, unsure of whether the path would be clear all the way to the road at Kinloch. It may have been wet and misty but it wasn't cold, and we hiked on, warm and dry in our cocoon of Gore-Tex waterproofs. It's often said that in hillwalking terms there is no such thing as bad weather, only bad clothing, and there is much truth in that.

It took us about three hours to walk the ten kilometres of the Moine Path, three hours in which we saw very little other than the green flow of the moor around us. This whole area, the peninsula of land between Loch Hope and the Kyle of Tongue, is known as A' Mhòine – the moss, or the peat. It's a boggy wilderness, home to golden plovers and dunlins, wheatears and skylarks, hen harriers and peregrines. Red deer herds roam here, drifting between the lochans but we saw very little of the wildlife or the scenery. The main Durness to Tongue road crosses the northern reaches of A' Mhòine, close to the coast, the most northerly and one of the loneliest stretches of road in the country. From its edge lie miles and miles of reddish, undulating moor that sweeps up to the flanks of Ben Hope.

Near this road you'll find the remains of the Moine House, a shelter for wayfarers, not quite a bothy but nothing as grand as a hotel or guest house. A wordy plaque still adorns the gable wall:

> *This road was made in the year 1830 and at the sole expense of the Marquis of Stafford. Those who feel not the delay nor experience the fatigue nor suffer from the risks and interruptions incident to the former state of the country can but slightly estimate the advantages of its present improved condition or what it cost to procure them.*
>
> *To mark this change – to note these facts – to record this date this inscription is put up and dedicated by James Loch Esq. MP, auditor and commissioner upon his Lordship's estates and John Horsburgh Esq, factor for the Reay Country, Strath Naver, Strathalladale and Assynt under whose directions this work was executed and who alone know the difficulties that occurred in its execution and liberality and perseverance by which they were overcome.*
>
> *Peter Lawson, Surveyor.*

We eventually came out of the cloud to be greeted by a forlorn and grey Kyle of Tongue. The multiple tops of Ben Loyal flirted with us through the mists, appearing and disappearing in the cloud. Past Kinloch Lodge we took the minor road for the final few kilometres to the start of the track that would take us to Ben Loyal. Or perhaps not …

The end of any long walk is a bitter-sweet experience, the sadness at the conclusion of what is, in most cases, a great experience offset by the simple pleasures of a hot shower and those little luxuries of life that are so often taken for granted.

Sometimes, just sometimes, the thought of those little luxuries can overwhelm us, especially when we are wet and a little cold, and that hot shower and a meal are only minutes away. In such circumstances it's tempting to cut the trip short and high-tail it back to that other life we belong to, the existence that enjoys comfortable beds, central heating, three-course meals and bottles of ice-cold Chardonnay.

Gina and I had crossed the Moine Path from Strath More in fairly miserable conditions. Low cloud had obscured the promised views of Ben Hope's northern crags, underfoot

Big, open skies are as much a distinctive feature of Sutherland as neighbouring Caithness. They are best appreciated, we think, with a wee dram in hand.

conditions were wet and often boggy and heavy showers had forced us into full waterproofs. On reaching the tarmac at Kinloch we knew we had six or seven kilometres on the road (albeit a quiet minor road), to Ribigill Farm and the route to Ben Loyal. We also knew this point would test our willpower. From there it would only be a few kilometres to journey's end at Tongue, and a comfortable hotel room with hot showers.

Ben Loyal, with its castellated ridge, is one of the distinctive landmarks of Sutherland's far north. Often called "The Queen of the Highlands", it is seen here from Lochan Hakel in early spring.

I rehearsed the route to the mountain in my mind. Follow the farm road south through the farm and onto the moors beyond. Splash over a boggy track past the empty buildings at Cunside and climb grassy slopes to the Bealach Clais nan Ceap, a wide flat pass that separates the main mountain from the outlier of Ben Heil, then climb steeper grassy slopes to gain the broad summit ridge between Sgòr Chaonasaid and An Caisteal. From here, the broad summit ridge leads to a large granite block. The summit trig point lies on top of this block. I knew it would be a wet and windy ascent, and views would be minimal. Was this the way we wanted to end what had been a fabulous journey through one of the most incredible landscapes in Europe?

Under such circumstances the mind goes into turmoil, playing the temptations of the flesh against the disciplines of the walk. From the Ribigill road end it's a fifteen kilometre round trip to the summit of Ben Loyal, which, by now, had black clouds swarming around its four summit tors. The weather looked unlikely to improve and, at the foot of a long uphill stretch of tarmac, my body and mind became inextricably linked. I suggested to Gina we bash on to the Tongue Hotel and leave Ben Loyal for another day. Her broad smile confirmed agreement.

I must admit to some feelings of guilt. A week before, we had climbed the eroded flanks of Suilven, convincing ourselves that the route began on the summit of the mountain, that this was a trans-Sutherland route from Suilven to Ben Loyal, and not from Lochinver to Tongue. I guess we were being a little fanciful, intoxicated by good weather and the prospect of a week's walking before us. At the time, it seemed like a nice idea and now, here we were, turning our backs on the final mountain of the trip, the alleged destination, the high point of the journey and its northern terminus. In our defence, we had both climbed the hill before, and I knew I would be returning within weeks to climb it again with a television crew. As it was, by the time we had checked in to the hotel – with a room, according to the receptionist, with the most wonderful view of Ben Loyal – the clouds had devoured all sight of the hill and the rain had taken on a new level of intensity. All traces of guilt vanished. We took a shower and headed for the bar …

BEN LOYAL

Two months later I returned with Richard and our producer Margaret, our cameraman Dominic and a safety officer, my old climbing pal John Lyall from Kincraig. Greylag geese grazed noisily in the fields of Ribigill Farm as we tramped south over waterlogged moors towards the golden flanks of Ben Loyal, its four summits still clear of cloud. Autumn had arrived in the far north and the world was golden.

Earlier we had driven down the road from Tongue for a short distance to Lochan Hakel, for it's here, across wind-ruffled waters, that Ben Loyal stands fortress-like, its castellated outline defined in four weather-worn turrets of granite. For sheer extravagance of form and shape Ben Loyal has few peers, its relatively lowly height exaggerated by its isolated position. Few would argue with the description of Ben Loyal as "the Queen of Scottish mountains" given in the *New Statistical Account* of 1840.

Cameron, a lone figure almost lost in the landscape, approaches the summit of Ben Loyal with the Kyle of Tongue in the background.

We had come to film the climax of the long television journey, which we had decided would be broken over the three seasons of spring, summer and autumn in an attempt to catch the colours and events of the seasons. If we had filmed later in the summer we would have been too late for the nesting seabirds on Handa Island, and if we had come in the spring we would have missed the golden aura of autumn, the sound of the rutting stags and the migrating geese.

In previous days of the shoot we had heard much about the history of the area, about the Strath Naver Clearances and older historical events which still resonate today. Throughout this northern region you'll find ancient tumuli, cup and ring marks, brochs and standing stones, and on an isolated islet at the southern end of Lochan Hakel lie the remains of a small fort called Grianan, reputedly a hunting lodge of the King of Norway. Elsewhere in the loch you might even find the remnants of a Jacobite treasure trove.

Arms and gold were sent from France in support of Charles Edward Stuart's Jacobite cause, but the ship was attacked several times, by both pirates and Government vessels, forcing the French sloop to sail north and into the treacherous waters of the Pentland Firth. With a Hanoverian frigate in hot pursuit the French ship ran aground in the Kyle of Tongue near Melness. The captain and crew managed to save much of the arms and the gold and set out to trek to Inverness, but they were attacked by Government-supporting Mackays. Rather than allow the booty to fall into the hands of the enemy, the Jacobites tossed the lot into the waters of Lochan Hakel – or so the story goes. It's been suggested that one local shepherd became suddenly wealthy, long before the days of the National Lottery …

A tint of that gold could well have been reflected on the slopes of Ben Loyal as we climbed up the grassy slopes from the old farm buildings at Cunside. Autumn had arrived in a riot of extravagant earth tones – gold, ochre, yellow and burnished bronze. Above us the steep crags of Sgòr Chaonasaid (712 metres) rose to a well-defined point and beyond it, above the Bealach Clais nan Ceap, steep grassy slopes led to a broad summit ridge, with Sgòr Chaonasaid at the north end and An Caisteal, the Corbett summit of the mountain at 765 metres, a kilometre to the south.

Throughout our ascent we had been entertained by the roaring of stags, defiantly defending their harem of hinds from marauding rivals. At one point we watched two stags run towards each other, intent on antlered battle, before one lost courage and veered off uphill, the other in hot pursuit. The deep-bellied roar of the rutting stag was impressive, one of the great sounds of the Highland hills, and was held sacred by the Celtic people who revered the stag for its sexual ability. One of the Celtic deities, Cernunnos, was always represented as a stag-antlered figure.

On the summit ridge, the roar of the deer was replaced by the roar of the wind, and the steep clamber up the granite block to the cairn was made a tad tricky by a gale that threatened to blow us back to Cunside. My final piece to camera – the climax of the hour-long documentary – was delivered as I clung tenaciously to the trig point, in mortal fear of being lifted up and blown away.

Time is rarely on your side when filming, so we didn't have the opportunity of climbing the hill's other tops but it's certainly worth doing so. To complete the walk, the best route is to continue south from An Caisteal over Beinn Bheag, or Heddle's Top as it's known, then onto Carn an Tionail. Return to Heddle's Top and follow its north-west ridge out to the sharper summit of Sgòr a'Chlèirich. Any descent to the north from this summit would be rather tricky so it's best to return along the ridge to the low point then drop down into the mountain's un-named north-west corrie where steep slopes will take you down to the birch woods of Coille na Cùile and an easy walk back towards the path near Cunside.

Journey's end at last. Cameron stands on the summit of Ben Loyal at the completion of the Sutherland Trail.

Looking back over the Sutherland Trail from the summit of Ben Loyal and the remote yet spectacular scenery that is typical of the whole trail.

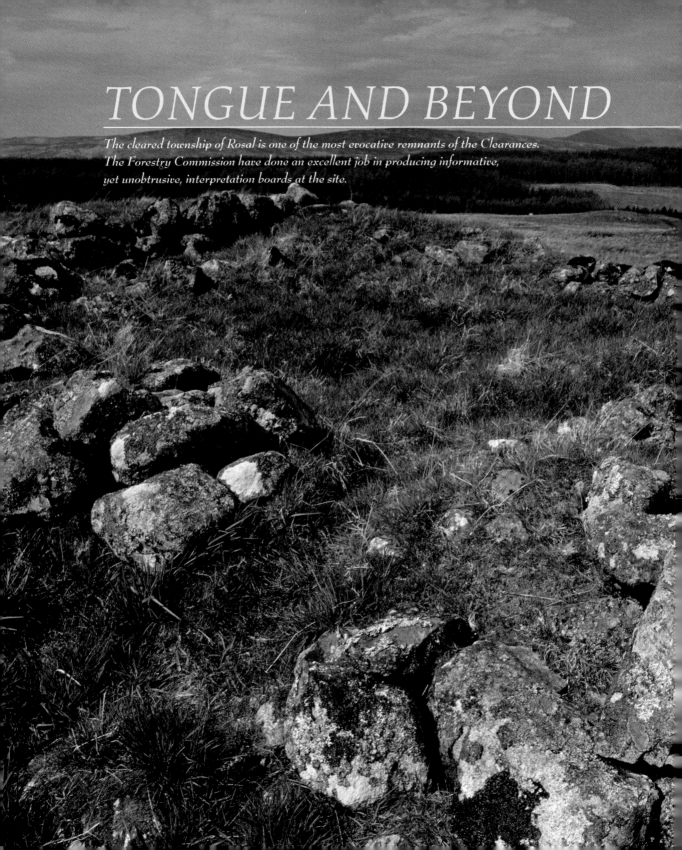

TONGUE AND BEYOND

The cleared township of Rosal is one of the most evocative remnants of the Clearances.
The Forestry Commission have done an excellent job in producing informative,
yet unobtrusive, interpretation boards at the site.

Happily ensconced in the Tongue Hotel with the comfort of a real bed instead of a sleeping bag and top quality food instead of endless pasta, Gina and I set about discovering something of the area around this northern village and the surrounding Mackay Country.

One of the main villages on the north coast of Sutherland, Tongue lies on the eastern side of the Kyle of Tongue, a large sea inlet that extends from Tongue Bay inland for about ten kilometres. The village is an important junction where the road from the south (from Altnaharra and Lairg) meets the north coast road that runs from Durness to Melvich and on to Caithness. This road crosses the Kyle of Tongue by means of a long sweeping causeway and bridge built in 1971. Before then, travellers either had to take the passenger ferry that crossed the Kyle, until this ceased to run in 1956, or drive the sixteen kilometres along the narrow road that runs round the head of the Kyle.

Tongue became the seat of the Clan Mackay in 1554 when their castle at Borve was destroyed by the Gordons of Sutherland. On the coast of their ancient province of Strath Naver, Tongue House was burnt in 1656 by Cromwellian forces but was rebuilt by the Master of Reay in 1678, and added to in the 18th century. In 1829 it had to be sold by the 7th Lord Reay, together with the vast Mackay estate (the whole north-western corner of Britain) to cover debts owed to the Sutherland family.

As well as Tongue House and Castle Borve, another Mackay stronghold is the 14th century Caisteal Bharraich (anglicised to Castle Varrich), which stands on the inlet overlooking the Kyle of Tongue. It's been suggested the castle was built on the foundations of a Norse fort, the stronghold of a Norse warrior of the 11th century. Some believe it could be the 'Beruvik' mentioned in the Norse *Orkneyinga Saga*. You can reach it via a signposted footpath that runs from the centre of Tongue.

Tradition suggests that the Bishops of Caithness used it when moving between Scrabster and Balnakiel House near Durness. It is said to be the oldest stone building in the north of Scotland and is built on Lewisian Gneiss, the oldest rock in the United Kingdom.

People have lived in this area for thousands of years and there are various Bronze and Iron Age sites nearby. The Norse settled in the area over 1,000 years ago; indeed the name Tongue derives from the Old Norse word 'Tunga', meaning 'a tongue of land'.

THE ANGLER: BRUCE SANDISON

The lochs, estuaries, rivers and hill lochans are all famous for the quality of their fishing and one man who knows more about that than anyone else is an old friend, Bruce Sandison, Scotland's best-known angler. A regular correspondent on a number of fishing magazines, Bruce wrote a weekly column on fishing in *The Scotsman* for well over a decade and he's the author of the highly respected *Trout Lochs of Scotland*.

Bruce and I once shared the same BBC Radio Scotland producer, Christopher Lowell, one of the best radio producers I ever worked with. Chris knew exactly what he wanted in terms of good material, and he wasn't slow in telling you if he thought you'd fallen short. I worked with him on a long-running weekly environmental

Doyen of fly fishermen and long-time campaigner against 'polluting fish farms', Bruce Sandison is also author of the definitive anglers' guide, Rivers and Lochs of Scotland.

magazine show called *In the Country*. It was through Chris that I learned a great deal about environmental and conservation politics and many aspects of land and wildlife management that I would never have learned as someone who just tramped the hills and scribbled one or two newspaper columns.

Before I began presenting *In The Country* for BBC Scotland I had put together a number of short ten-minute broadcasts called *Tales of the Hills,* which went out after the news on a Friday evening, and the standard I had to meet had been set by an angler from Caithness by the name of Bruce Sandison.

His series *Tales of the Loch*, also produced by Chris, was fascinating and made me realise early on that trout fishermen and hillwalkers were very similar in outlook. Just as I wandered the hills to enjoy the solitude, the wildlife and the simple beauty of the natural world, so it was with fishermen, many of whom were happy to simply be there on the shore of some remote loch in the Highlands, casting their flies on the water, not really caring if they caught a fish or not.

I hadn't seen Bruce for some fifteen years or so. We had once spent an evening at a rather curious Hogmanay-style party in an old farmhouse near Kincardine O'Neil in Aberdeenshire, the home of the broadcaster Freda Morrison. The idea was that the party would be full of outdoor types and it would be recorded and broadcast on the radio at New Year as a kind of outdoors Hogmanay Special. I can't remember all that much about it, other than that I drank too much and Bruce reminded me that it was a very strange evening indeed. I guess any party that pretends it's a Hogmanay party about a month before the actual event is bound to feel rather odd. It reminded me of those very curious Turkey and Tinsel weekends that some Highland hotels put on in September. Coachloads of pensioners from Todmorden or Leeds come to the Highlands and celebrate Christmas on the Friday evening then go for a Hogmanay bash on the Saturday. They probably roll Easter eggs on the Sunday!

Bruce Sandison has lived in the north of Scotland for almost 35 years. He and I have enjoyed a similar career path, both leaving the Central Belt to tuck ourselves away in the Highlands where we have tried to earn a living writing about those activities we loved best; in my case, mountaineering and hillwalking and in Bruce's case, trout and salmon fishing.

I asked him how he first became interested in angling and he replied succinctly: "Rugby." He had a look of distaste on his craggy face. "I found myself lying face down in the mud with a dozen other guys jumping on top of me just because I happened to be lying on an oval ball. I decided there and then that rugby wasn't for me. My father then encouraged me to try golf but that didn't appeal either. We then tried fishing and that was it. I remember going down to the Water of Leith and seeing these little things swim around in the water below me. That was it. I wanted to catch them, touch them, examine them. They were beautiful and I think that was the defining moment."

No-one in Bruce's family fished so he was introduced to an older couple who ran a newsagent in Edinburgh who took the young Sandison under their wing and taught him the dark secrets of trout fishing. He never looked back.

After a spell in the army and a number of years working in industry in Edinburgh, Bruce decided to move north to the land of his ancestors. His mother's folks had come from Caithness so that's where Bruce, with his wife Ann and young family, turned his face. He was going to spend his life fishing and wandering the wild areas of Scotland and he was going to earn a crust or two by writing about it. The bold optimism of youth.

I remember taking the same decision, faced with providing for a very patient wife and two young sons, in my early thirties. We had been running youth hostels for the SYHA for a number of years and I was spending spare time writing features for newspapers and magazines and writing books. Eventually I took the plunge and decided to write about mountains on a full-time basis. It was uncannily like the track that Bruce Sandison found himself on.

"It was interesting in those days that we were seen as incomers, despite the fact that I had relatives in Caithness, but that didn't worry me unduly. That's something that happens all over the country, not just in Caithness or Sutherland. I wasn't local. End of story, but it was never a problem. Even now, after living in the north for almost 35 years, I'm still probably regarded as an incomer but those attitudes are changing as more and more people are moving north and settling in these areas."

In this landscape boats are often a better way to travel than on the winding roads.

After seventeen years in Caithness, Bruce moved west to Tongue in Sutherland, into an old farmhouse on the side of a hill overlooking the Kyle of Tongue. The castellated form of Ben Loyal dominates the view from his sitting room window. By the time he moved to Tongue he was an established and well-respected writer with a number of books under his belt, including the very popular *Trout Lochs of Scotland*, the third edition of which was published not long after we met. That is probably Bruce's most successful book, although his son described it as "the greatest work of fiction ever written."

> **" The place is full of eagles, and buzzards, and hawks and deer and foxes and wildcat and all kinds of birds. "**

But what was so special about Sutherland to make Bruce Sandison stay there? Is there nowhere else in the world he'd rather live?

"It's the space, the big skies, the wildlife, the hills, the lack of people and of course the trout lochs and salmon rivers. People call Sutherland the empty lands but that's nonsense. The place is full of eagles, and buzzards, and hawks and deer and foxes and wildcat and all kinds of birds. I have a keen enthusiasm for ornithology and I love to walk the hills in all their seasons. Indeed, my wife Ann and I love nothing more than taking a long walk, perhaps visiting five lochs, where we can enjoy a bit of fishing in each of them. It makes a grand excuse for a walk …"

But what of the future? Does Bruce see Sutherland changing very much in the near future as more and more people leave city life behind them and move north?

"I don't really know," said Bruce, "and I'm not sure I really care. I can't see it changing very much in my lifetime and provided the hills and the birds and the fishing are still all here I'll be happy."

Bruce and I spent a day on Loch Haluim, a remote loch below the southern slopes of Ben Loyal. As we gazed down on the butterfly-shaped outline of the loch from the shoulder of the hill it was obvious why Bruce loved wild landscapes like this. From the hillside we gazed across at Ben Klibreck and Ben Hope, Scotland's two most northerly Munros, and to the south lay Ben Hee giving way to the complex geology of Arkle and Foinaven and the mountains created by the Moine Thrust. These are magical names to hillwalkers, and to be in the heart of them in this wild and remote land was good enough for me, but Bruce wanted more. He wanted to catch some fish.

Bruce's son-in-law Ian, the keeper on the Ben Loyal Estate, had kindly brought a rowing boat up for us the day before so we organised the fishing rods and flies, pushed off from a small sandy bay and drifted out into the loch, Bruce correcting my rarely used casting techniques. We were only on the water a few minutes when Bruce had his first catch, a lovely golden-hued brown trout. Soon he was pulling them in willy-nilly, while I was too busy blethering to Bruce to notice the little tugs on my line that would indicate a fish was interested in my lure. At one point, thinking that Bruce wasn't fully concentrating on the conversation, I asked him if he was actually watching the water for fish. "Like a hawk," was his curt reply!

Those few hours we enjoyed on the loch gave me an insight into the peace and tranquillity that trout fishing holds for people. Despite the attitude of many conservationists, who see fishing in the same light as deer stalking or hare coursing, I couldn't see Bruce as a hunter. There may have been some kind of hunter–gatherer instinct at play in his psyche but he was obviously content just to be there, at one with the environment, catching the little trout and then releasing them back to the dark waters of the loch. (Later, when asked how many fish we had caught, Bruce very diplomatically said the boat had pulled in ten – he caught them all, I got barely a nibble.)

When I asked him if he considered himself a hunter, he gave me a withering look and shook his head. Could he take a gun and stalk and shoot a red deer stag, for example? He simply shook his head again, and yet Bruce is more than aware of the politics of the countryside, more than aware that people like his son-in-law Ian have to meet Red Deer Commission targets for the reduction of deer numbers here on Ben Loyal Estate. If wealthy individuals are happy to pay large sums of money to hunt, and this helps the keepers and stalkers manage deer numbers, then why not? Such an income is vital in remote communities like this one, and keeps people like Ian and his family living and working on the land, alongside those other folk who have moved here to enjoy other aspects of the environment, people like Bruce Sandison.

THE OYSTER FARMER: ANGELA MACKAY

Sutherland is reinventing itself. People are returning to the glens, not in great numbers yet, but as the tensions and strife of urban Britain become increasingly intolerable, more and more people are searching for an alternative lifestyle. Angela Mackay, the short cheery woman we met on the foreshore of the Kyle of Tongue, is one such person. Angela is a former hairdresser turned oyster farmer, and we filmed her as she was hauling some strange looking net bags behind her.

Grown organically on the side of the Kyle of Tongue, in some of Britain's purest waters, Angela Mackay's oysters are the only ones classed as grade A all year round.

Angela farms succulent Pacific oysters in the crystal-clear waters of the Kyle of Tongue. But twenty years ago Angela was cutting hair and giving blue rinses and perms to the womenfolk of Bettyhill. Her transformatory moment took place when she went along to a talk about oyster farming in the local school. From that moment she became infatuated with the idea of farming oysters. She sold her hairdressing business and set up a new enterprise, close to her home in Melness, growing Pacific oysters under the brand name of Kyle of Tongue Oysters.

Angela would claim that her change of profession was spurred by the fact that oysters don't talk back to you but after only a few hours in her cheerful company I learned more facts about these molluscs than I knew existed. Did you know that oysters have a three-chambered heart, colourless blood and a pair of kidneys; or that they change sex – these 'protandrous alternating hermaphrodites' start off life as males producing sperm then switch to egg-producing females and can then switch back to being males again? Or that Roman Emperors paid for them by their weight in gold? It is said that Henry IV liked to toss back 300 as an appetiser and that Casanova reportedly consumed 50–60 oysters a day with his evening punch.

Perhaps, after my long walk, I looked a bit undersexed, so Angela kindly gave me a bag of oysters for my supper, and the chef in the Tongue Hotel, Grant McNicol, prepared them for me and showed me how to 'slurp' them out of the shell. I couldn't have had a better teacher. The previous year Grant was Scottish Young Chef of the Year and he took great delight in telling me that he had no wish to ply his trade anywhere other than in Scotland.

"With some of the best seafood in the world, beef and lamb from the Castle of Mey Estate in Caithness and venison fresh off the hill, this area has some of the best produce in the world. Why would I want to work in somewhere like Edinburgh or London?"

Angela Mackay talks through the finer points of eating oysters. She says you shouldn't be snobbish, grilling them with cheese is fine!

THE SHEPHERD: JAN MACKENZIE

Grant's was a fair question. Just as Angela and Grant are delighted to earn a living from the land and the sea, others have discovered a satisfying lifestyle in more traditional pursuits – like shepherding. Jan Mackenzie was born and brought up on a croft on Strath Naver and is one of Scotland's few female shepherds. She now owns her own croft and has recently bought a second one. She also works as the shepherd on the North Loch Naver Estate. She receives a wage for this work but her salary also depends on the price she gets for the sheep at the Lairg sales.

Before the sales, she took time to show me her flock of tups and there was no mistaking the sense of pride in her voice as she pointed out the various features and characteristics that make a potential champion tup. The flock of North Cheviots looked as though they'd all been through a washing machine, specially spruced up for the television cameras. They were snow white and spotless, far removed from the shaggy, dirty creatures we're used to seeing on the hills.

Despite the hard times and low lamb prices of recent years, the sheep market at Lairg is still one of the biggest in Europe. The market represents the moment of reckoning for the year's income for people like Jan Mackenzie.

We filmed Jan at the sheep sales where she was pleased with the prices she was getting for the sheep. This was the culmination of her year's work, both physically and financially. She was particularly happy with the prices reached for the estate sheep, and, with bidding going well, she was hopeful that she would do even better than she had expected before the sales.

One of the things that I had noticed on my journey through Sutherland was the comparative lack of sheep. A few years ago you would have seen sheep grazing at every corner, eating virtually everything that had the temerity to grow from the ground. But many of these northern estates have now been given over almost exclusively to sporting purposes – fly fishing, grouse shooting and deer stalking – with visitors willing to pay considerable amounts of money to come here and participate in such activities. Having said that, few would disagree that sheep farming is still vital to the Highland economy.

Lairg auction mart boasts the largest one-day sheep sale in the UK. The prices raised here are a barometer of the livestock market in the far north.

In her lifetime Jan has seen a big reduction in the number of shepherds working these northern hills. "There used to be four or five shepherds on each estate," she told me, "and now there will be one, if any at all."

So how important are sheep on a landscape like this, I asked, sweeping my arm around the low lying hills of Strath Naver.

Shepherd Jan Mackenzie sorts her sheep into the right pens at the auction mart. The animals are specially groomed for this all-important day.

"They're very important," she replied, with a look that said she thought it was a pretty stupid question. "I mean, there's a lot of sheep gone from here anyway, but if you lose the sheep from the land it's going to change the whole environment. The ground vegetation will get rank, it'll grow long and choke everything and if the ground isn't grazed hard enough, it'll change everything. We do need sheep on the land …"

I'm delighted to report that Jan was fairly happy with what she earned at the Lairg sales and I hope that will allow her to continue in her age-old profession that she so obviously loves. I think most of us who go to the hills would miss the sheep if they had to go – they're part and parcel of the hill scene in Scotland. Without them to keep the bracken and long grasses under control, the underfoot conditions for us hillwalkers would become pretty difficult, but it's ironic that it was the introduction of sheep that was the driving force in the notorious Strath Naver Clearances of 200 years ago.

THE STRATH NAVER CLEARANCES

Early in the 19th century, there were over 50 townships in Strath Naver alone and the area received widespread publicity when the Gaelic speaking population was thrown out to make way for commercial sheep farming.

Bettyhill school head teacher Jim Johnston has spent years studying the Strath Naver Clearances. He took me down a long forest track into what was the old village of Rosal, an atmospheric spot of rumpled hillocks and flat meadows where the corrugated lines of old lazy beds – where the soil has been piled into long, narrow, raised mounds which were used to grow vegetables – were still visible. A few ruckles of stone were scattered about and it took little imagination to see them as low walls and gable ends, supporting roofs of turf through which smoke wafted from the family fire inside.

We stepped over the fallen rocks into what would once have been a family home, with a byre attached.

"Prior to the Clearances," Jim told me, "this would have been a substantial house. Most of the space would have been taken up by cattle, and for that reason these houses were

Bettyhill head teacher and local historian Jim Johnston was Cameron's knowledgeable guide to the Clearances in Strath Naver.

often built on a slope, with the cattle down at the lower end so that the effluent they produced during the winter months would flow away from the house, rather than up into the kitchen area.

"It was a time when opportunity was available for anyone who had any kind of entrepreneurial spirit. And the Countess of Sutherland certainly had that spirit in abundance. As did Patrick Sellar, her factor, or estate manager."

In the early 19th century, the Sutherland family owned immense properties – "an area unequalled in the British Empire" and the Duke of Sutherland had already significantly 'modernised' his vast estates in Staffordshire. He and his wife were determined to make the Sutherland estate more productive and financially rewarding. They were advised to move the people away from Strath Naver, Strathbrora and the Strath of Kildonan and to turn these areas into huge sheep farms. The evicted people would be given allotments on the coast, as Patrick Sellar wrote:

> Lord and Lady Stafford were pleased humanely to order the new arrangement of this country. That the interior should be possessed by Cheviot shepherds, and the people brought down to the coast and placed in lots of less than three acres, sufficient for the maintenance of an industrious family, pinched enough to cause them to turn their attention to the fishing.
>
> A most benevolent action, to put these barbarous Highlanders into a position where they could better associate together, apply themselves to industry, educate their children, and advance in civilisation.

History hasn't been particularly kind to Patrick Sellar, recording him as an evictor, a cruel factor who burnt the grazings so there would be no food for the cattle, and who appeared to take delight in marching the inhabitants of Strath Naver down to the coastal fringes where they were allocated marked-out plots of land to build new homes. These fringes were often rocky and desolate, and many of the evicted chose to emigrate rather than starve on the shores of Sutherland.

However, Jim Johnston suggests that the element of cruelty, or viciousness on Sellar's part has been slightly exaggerated.

"There is no recording of people's houses being burnt around them in Rosal," he told me, "and no-one died directly from the evictions, but nevertheless Patrick Sellar has always come across as a villain, and that continues even today – it would be a very dangerous thing to do to go into a bar in Bettyhill and praise Patrick Sellar.

"He had absolutely no compunction in evicting people from ground that he possessed or anything like that. He knew what he wanted and he was prepared to pursue it with very little regard for other people.

"He was one of the largest farmers in the whole of Scotland and in that area, the area of his one farm, there had been 2,000 people living, prior to the Clearances. And these 2,000 people were replaced by eighteen shepherds from the Borders. But from the point of view of Victorian society he was a big success and was, undoubtedly, an expert farmer. But then Mussolini made the Italian trains run on time."

Although Patrick Sellar may not have burnt down cottages in Rosal village, he appeared to have done so elsewhere. Reverend Donald Sage, a church missionary, lived at the time across Loch Naver at Achness. In his book, *Memorabilia Domestica*, published in 1889, the minister paints a dark picture of the times.

> *To my poor and defenceless flock the dark hour of trial came in right earnest. It was the month of April 1819 that they were all – man, woman and child – from the Heights of Farr to the mouth of the Naver, on one day to quit their tenements and go – many of them knew not whither. For a few, some miserable patches of ground along the shore were doled as lots without anything in the shape of the poorest hut to shelter them. Upon these lots it was decided that they should build houses at their own expense, and cultivate the ground, at the same time occupying themselves as fishermen, although the great majority of them had never set foot in a boat in their lives.*

> *At an early hour on a Tuesday, Mr Sellar, escorted by a large body of constables, sheriff-officers and others, commenced work at Grummore, the first inhabited township to the west. They gave the inmates half an hour to pack up and carry off their furniture, and then set the cottages on fire. To this plan they ruthlessly adhered. The roofs and rafters were lighted up into one red blaze.*

I had occasion the next week to visit the manse of Tongue. On my way thither, I passed through the scene of the campaign of burning. Of all the houses, the thatched roofs were gone; but the walls remained. The flames of the preceding week still slumbered in their ruins, and sent up into the air spiral columns of smoke. The sooty rafters of the cottages as they were being consumed, filled the air with a heavy and most offensive odour. Nothing could more vividly represent the horrors of grinding oppression.

History has a curious habit of repeating itself, and I think one of the most telling things about the Highland Clearances is that similarly cruel events are still going on in various parts of the world. There are still places where traditional lifestyles are being disrupted and destroyed. I couldn't help but recall television images of people being displaced during the Balkan wars of the 1990s, or the atrocities of Rwanda and Darfur.

Today there is an interpretive leaflet for the walk to Rosal (written by Jim Johnston) and it's good that we don't forget such events. Indeed, for those who spend time on Scotland's hills and wild places, it's difficult to forget – the remaining ruins remind us that people once lived in these glens, glens that many people today describe as 'Europe's last wilderness'.

THE EMPTY LANDS NO MORE?

But what of Sutherland's reputation as 'the empty lands'? In the course of my journey between Lochinver and Tongue there is little doubt that much of the land is wild and unpopulated, magnificently so, but it is the grandeur of such landscapes that is attracting people to this north-west corner of Scotland. It was fascinating to talk to cavers, sea kayakers, anglers, climbers and hillwalkers who all described this far north-western corner of Scotland as one of the UK's great 'adventure destinations'.

More and more walkers are discovering the delights of Sutherland, the low-level walking routes as well as the more challenging hill routes. Sea kayakers have described the western coasts as some of the finest kayaking regions in the country. Scotland boasts very few decent sporting cave systems but the caves at Inchnadamph are being slowly developed and are attracting more and more visitors.

Sudden rain showers blowing in from the west produced this rainbow above the cleared village of Rosal.

In the time we spent in Sutherland filming the television programme that this book is taken from, we noticed a big increase in those camping in the various camp sites, particularly in places like Scourie and Durness. The fact that there are now some excellent hotels in the area, serving top-class meals from local produce, suggests that people are now prepared to drive from the south and expect a decent standard of accommodation and sustenance.

Add to that the field sportsmen, to whom this area will always be some kind of Shangri-La, and the anglers, both trout and salmon fishermen, who regard Sutherland as one of the finest fishing areas in the world, and the future of this old county as a sporting and recreation destination is secure.

But I think it was the people of Sutherland who had the biggest influence on me, and will encourage me to return time and time again. Those who are native to Sutherland and work on the land or in the service industries, and those who have moved here from the south, like Bruce Sandison and geologist Donald Fisher, who have both put down deep roots here and have no intention of moving anywhere else.

My experience of Sutherland is that we should never refer to it as the 'empty lands' and that this is a place of enormous promise and potential, where the past runs deep and where history, as in land reform, is still being made. It's a land of contrasts, between a rugged, cliff-lined coastline to the gentle Flow Country that ripples its way east from Ben Loyal into Caithness; from the high tops of some of the most incredible mountains in the land to the white sandy beaches of Assynt and Durness. And the finest way to appreciate these contrasts, the best way to experience the heartbeat and beauty of the land, is to walk through it. Try following the Sutherland Trail. I commend it to you with a passion.

The end of a perfect day as the sun sets off the west coast of Sutherland with the Hebrides silhouetted on the horizon.

GAELIC GLOSSARY

aber, abhair river's mouth, occasionally a confluence

abhainn river

achadh field, plain or meadow

aird height, high point

airidh shieling

aonach ridge

ath ford

ban, bhan white, bright, fair

beag small

bealach pass, col or saddle

beith birch

ben, beinn, benn hill, mountain

bidean peak

bodach old man

braigh brae, hill-top

breac speckled

brochan porridge

buachaille shepherd, herdsman, guardian

buidhe yellow

buiridh bellowing, roaring

cailleach old woman

camas bay

carn cairn, pile of stones

cas step

ceann head

choinnich mossy place, bog

chrois cross or crossing place

ciche pap, nipple

cill cell, church

ciste chest, coffin

clach stony

clachan township

cnoc hillock

coille wood

coire, choire corrie, cwm

creachan rock

creag crag, cliff

croit croft

cruach, chruach hill

cuach cup, deep hollow

cul back

dail field

damh, daimh stag

darach oakwood

dearg red, pink

diollaid saddle

diridh a divide

dorus strait, gate

drochaid bridge

drum, druim ridge

dubh dark, black

dun fort, stronghold

each horse

eagach notched place

eas waterfall

eighe file, notched

eileach rock

eilean island

eun bird

fada, fhada long

fearn alder

fiadh deer

fionn white, fair

frith deer forest

fuar cold

gabhar goat

gaoth, gaoith wind

garbh rough

garbhanach rough ridge

gartain enclosed field

geal white

gearanach walled ridge

gearr short

gille young man, boy

glais burn

glas, ghlais grey, green

gleann glen

glomach chasm

gorm   blue

innis, inch   meadow, sometimes island

inver, inbhir   confluence

iolair   eagle

kin   head

knock, cnoc   hillock

kyle   strait

ladhar   forked, hoofed

lagan   hollow

lairig   pass

laoigh   calf

laroch   dwelling place

leac   slab, stone

leathad   slope

leis   lee, leeward

leitir   slope

liath   grey

lochan   small lake

maighdean, mhaighdean   maiden

mairg   rust coloured

mam   rounded hill

maol, mull   headland, bare hill

meadhoin   middle

meall   round hill

moin, mhoin, moine   bog, moss, peat

monadh   heathery hill

mor, mhor   big

muc, muice   pig

mullach   top summit

odhar   dun coloured

ord   conical hill

poite   pot

poll   pool, pit

puist   post

righ   king

ros, ross   promontory, moor

ruadh   red

rubha, rudha   point, promontory

ruigh   shieling

sail   heel

sean, sin   old

seileach   willow

sgeir   reef

sgiath   wing

sgurr, sgorr   sharp pointed peak

sith   fairy

sithean   fairy hill

spidean   peak

sron   nose

stac   steep rock, cliff, sea stack

steall   waterfall

stob   peak

suidhe   seat

tarmachan   ptarmigan

teallach   forge, hearth

tigh   house

tir   area, region, land

tobar   well

tom   hill

torr   small hill

tulach, tulachan   hillock

uaine   green

uamh   cave

uig   bay

uisge   water

SUGGESTED READING

General

The Undiscovered Country, Phil Bartlett. Ernest Press, 1993. A bold and fascinating attempt which looks beyond the dreams and aspirations of mountain lovers to ask the simple questions – what is the attraction of hills and mountains, and why should we want to climb them?

Hamish's Mountain Walk, Hamish Brown. Gollancz, 1977. The much-loved narrative of the first non-stop round of Scotland's Munros. The original Munro-bagger's guide.

The Last Hundred: Munros, Beards and a Dog, Hamish Brown. Mainstream Publishing, 1994. A series of essays on the hills of Scotland which ask some intriguing questions about how we look after our wild places.

Sacred Mountains: Ancient Wisdom and Modern Meanings, Adrian Cooper. Floris Books, 1997. Another book that asks the eternal question – why do we climb mountains? Cooper looks specifically at the sacred aspect of mountains, where many have experienced a spiritual dimension that has often changed their lives.

Landmarks: Exploration of Great Rocks, David Craig. Jonathan Cape, 1995. David Craig is a man with a heart for the land. This book examines the significance of great rocks, cliffs and outcrops and the influence they have over those who climb them or live near them.

On the Crofter's Trail: In Search of the Clearance Highlanders, David Craig. Jonathan Cape, 1997. The agony of the Clearances and the crofters' epic migration to Canada is the subject of this remarkable book.

Scottish Hill Names: Their Origin and Meaning, Peter Drummond. Scottish Mountaineering Trust, 2007. A must for anyone interested in the mountain names of Scotland. A fascinating piece of research that also includes phonetic pronunciations of all the Gaelic names.

Highways and Byways in the West Highlands, Seton Gordon. Birlinn, 1995. This is a revised edition of the original 1935 classic work. Seton Gordon was one of the great outdoor writers of the 20th century. A walker, naturalist and piper, he straddled the worlds of the recreational hillgoer and the professional naturalist.

The Wild Places, Robert Macfarlane. Granta Books, 2008. A superb treatise on wildness. Beautiful and intelligent.

Magic Mountains, Rennie McOwan. Mainstream Publishing, 1996. A superbly researched collection of tales of odd happenings in the hills. Not a book to be read when solo backpacking on long, dark, winter nights.

Mountaineering in Scotland and Undiscovered Scotland, W. H. Murray. Diadem Books, 1979. The books that launched several thousand mountaineering careers combined in a single edition. Classic accounts of pre-war mountaineering and hillwalking expeditions in Scotland written by Scotland's most articulate mountain writer.

Spirits of Place, Jim Perrin. Gomer Press, 1997. A powerful collection of essays, mostly on Wales, that describe the spirit of the people and the places held dear to the author, easily Britain's finest outdoor writer.

The Living Mountain, Nan Shepherd. Aberdeen University Press, 1977; reprinted Canongate, 2008. A celebration of the Cairngorms that contains some of the most insightful observations on these mountains I've ever read.

The Munros and Tops: A Record-Setting Walk in the Scottish Highlands, Chris Townsend. Mainstream Publishing, 1997. An account of the first continuous traverse of all Scotland's Munros and Tops.

The Scottish Lochs, Tom Weir. Constable, 1970. A superbly researched description of Scotland's major lochs and many of the hills that rise beside them.

Biophilia, E. O. Wilson. Harvard University Press, 1984. An eloquent statement of the conservation ethic. Wilson claims biophilia is the essence of our humanity, a state that binds us to all living species.

The North-West Highlands

The Northern Highlands: The Empty Lands, by Tom Atkinson. Luath Press, 2007. A guide to Wester Ross, Caithness and Sutherland.

The North-West Highlands, Dave Broadhead, Alec Keith and Ted Maden. Scottish Mountaineering Trust, 2004. An extremely useful hillwalking guide to the whole of the North-West Highlands.

Sutherland: An Archaeological Guide, Robert Gourlay. Birlinn, 1996. The first volume of two books on the historic sites and monuments of the north of Scotland.

The Chambered Cairns of Sutherland: An Inventory of the Structures and Their Contents, A. S. Henshall and J. N. G. Ritchie. Edinburgh University Press, 1995. A fascinating academic insight into the history of Sutherland.

Tongue and Farr, Jim A Johnston. J. A. Johnston, 1997. A fascinating account of the history of this northern part of Sutherland.

A Hillwalker's Guide to Sutherland: 22 great climbs in the far north of Scotland, Tom Strang. Sutherland Tourist Board, 1993. A very useful guide for hillgoers.

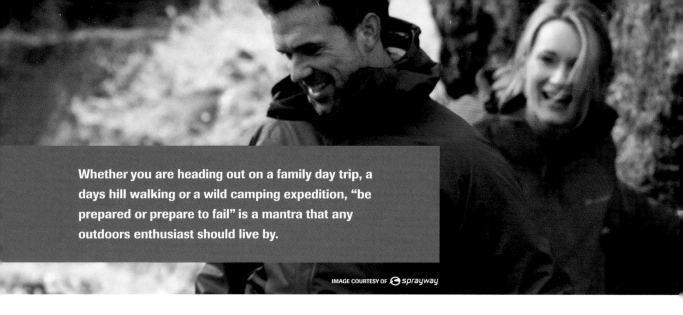

Whether you are heading out on a family day trip, a days hill walking or a wild camping expedition, "be prepared or prepare to fail" is a mantra that any outdoors enthusiast should live by.

In Scotland top of the list – after insect repellent – is waterproof clothing and footwear. The weather is as unpredictable as the scenery is beautiful and your experience can be ruined in one torrential downpour. The real question is what to buy to guarantee a dry day out? Every store in the Highlands has rails of 'waterproof' items to choose from. The choice is baffling, as are the differences in price – cheap in this case is not always cheerful.

One name that is particularly synonymous with waterproof clothing is the GORE-TEX® brand. A lot of people mistakenly believe that the company makes waterproof clothing. In fact, they make waterproof membranes that are used under license by clothing, shoe and accessory companies. You don't see the membrane as it is sandwiched to or bonded between outer fabrics and inner linings, but don't underestimate the value of GORE-TEX® products on a rainy day in Scotland!

The reasons why so many companies choose to use GORE-TEX® product technology is pretty straight forward – quality and performance. GORE-TEX® garments and footwear undergo the most stringent testing possible to ensure that they maintain the brand's promise GUARANTEED TO KEEP YOU DRY™. Quite a claim, but a proven claim because every element that makes up a finished GORE-TEX® product has to prove its excellence.

In the lab, the garments are put through more stress than you can ever inflict upon them before finally reaching the Gore Rain Chamber where they are battered by the elements. This makes sure that all of the zips, cuffs and seams are waterproof too. Also in the lab, GORE-TEX® footwear is subjected to "walking" in water for many miles to ensure all the components work together to keep water out. The shoes are also tested for "breathability in a special climate chamber. Once the garments and footwear have passed these tests they are sent out for field tests with people, like mountain instructors, whose work puts them in the most extreme weather conditions. This ensures that the products are fit for purpose and perform just as well on the hills as they do in the lab.

So how do GORE-TEX® products work? The porous structure of the GORE-TEX® membrane holds the secret to its success. Each pore in the membrane is about 20,000 times smaller than a drop of water, which stops any water getting in. The pores are also 700 times bigger than a water vapour molecule, which means that sweat and moisture can easily escape. This design keeps you dry and controls your body's temperature.

There are four different classes of GORE-TEX® fabric used in garments and three product classes for

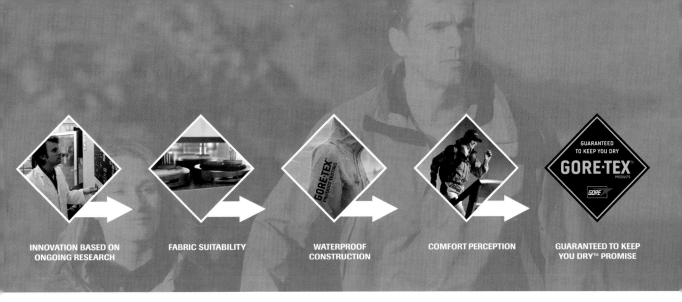

INNOVATION BASED ON ONGOING RESEARCH   FABRIC SUITABILITY   WATERPROOF CONSTRUCTION   COMFORT PERCEPTION   GUARANTEED TO KEEP YOU DRY™ PROMISE

GORE-TEX® footwear each of which is designed for different types of activity and conditions. In garments GORE-TEX® Soft Shell is constructed using soft, warm fabrics and is the ideal choice when freedom of movement is important in sports such as climbing, cycling and snowsports. GORE-TEX® Pro Shell is the most rugged, breathable and durable option and is designed for serious enthusiasts who experience the most extreme conditions. GORE-TEX® Paclite® Shell is used to create extremely lightweight, packable outerwear for activities like hiking, cycling and running, when weight and space are critical. GORE-TEX® Performance Shell is ideal for a wide range of outdoor activities, including skiing, cycling, mountaineering or just walking.

For footwear there is GORE-TEX® Extended Comfort Footwear, ideal for running, trail running and low level scrambling, GORE-TEX® Performance Comfort Footwear, ideal for hiking, trekking and hillwalking, GORE-TEX® Insulated Comfort Footwear, ideal for expedition trekking and high alpine climbing. All of these product classes carry the GUARANTEED TO KEEP YOU DRY™ promise.

Remember- stopping water from getting in your shoes and allowing sweat vapour to pass out of your shoes greatly reduces the chances of blisters – which significantly increases your chances of a great day out on the hill!

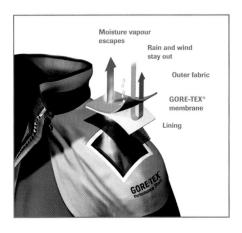

The important thing to remember when choosing any equipment for the outdoors is that you can't control the environment, but by having the right kit you can control its effect upon you. Choosing the right clothing and footwear is just as important as having the right tent, pack or poles and when quality is important GORE-TEX® garments and footwear will not let you down.

INDEX

LEAVE NO TRACE

The American **Leave No Trace** programme is a successful project to promote responsible outdoor recreation. It uses a simple set of principles which help minimise our impact on the environment we value and enjoy. These principles include:

1 Plan ahead and prepare
- ⇒ Prepare for extreme weather, hazards, and emergencies.
- ⇒ Schedule your trip to avoid times of high use.
- ⇒ Visit in small groups. Split larger parties into groups of four to six people.

2 Travel and camp on durable surfaces
In popular areas:
- ⇒ use existing paths and campsites
- ⇒ walk in single file in the middle of the path, even when wet or muddy
- ⇒ keep campsites small. Focus activity in areas where vegetation is absent.

In pristine areas:
- ⇒ disperse use to prevent the creation of campsites and paths
- ⇒ avoid places where impacts are just beginning.

Protect water sources by camping at least 50 metres from lochs and burns.

Good campsites are found, not made. Altering a site is not necessary.

3 Dispose of waste properly
- ⇒ Pack it in, pack it out. Inspect your campsite and rest areas for trash or spilled foods. Pack out all trash, leftover food, and litter.
- ⇒ Deposit solid human waste in catholes dug fifteen to twenty centimetres deep at least 50 metres from water, camp, and trails. Cover and disguise the cathole when finished.
- ⇒ Pack out toilet paper and hygiene products.
- ⇒ To wash yourself or your dishes, carry water 50 metres away from streams or lakes and use small amounts of biodegradable soap. Scatter strained dishwater.

4 Leave what you find
- ⇒ Preserve the past: examine, but do not touch, cultural or historic structures and artifacts.
- ⇒ Leave rocks, plants and other natural objects as you find them.

5 Minimise campfire impacts
- ⇒ Use a lightweight stove for cooking and enjoy a candle lantern for light.
- ⇒ If you do have a campfire, keep them small. Only use sticks from the ground that can be broken by hand.
- ⇒ Burn all wood and coals to ash, put out campfires completely, then scatter cool ashes.

6 Respect wildlife
- ⇒ Observe wildlife from a distance. Do not follow or approach them.
- ⇒ Never feed animals.
- ⇒ Control pets at all times, or leave them at home.
- ⇒ Avoid wildlife during sensitive times: mating, nesting, raising young, or winter.

7 Be considerate of other visitors
- ⇒ Respect other visitors and protect the quality of their experience.
- ⇒ Be courteous. Yield to other users on the trail.
- ⇒ Let nature's sounds prevail. Avoid loud voices and noises.

You can learn more at the **Leave No Trace** website at www.LNT.org.